FIGHTING SHAME
WITH THE WORD OF GOD

ASHAMED

SCARLET HILTIBIDAL

Lifeway Press®
Brentwood, Tennessee

Published by Lifeway Press® • © 2023 Scarlet Hiltibidal

ISBN: 978-1-0877-8751-0
Item: 005842771
Dewey decimal classification: 248.843
Subject heading: RELIGION / CHRISTIAN MINISTRY / YOUTH

To order additional copies of this resource, write Lifeway Resources Customer Service; 200 Powell Place, Suite 100; Brentwood, TN 37027-7707; FAX order to 615.251.5933; call toll-free 800.458.2772; email orderentry@lifeway.com; or order online at lifeway.com.

Printed in the United States of America

Lifeway Resources
200 Powell Place, Suite 100
Brentwood, TN 37027-7707

EDITORIAL TEAM,
LIFEWAY GIRLS

BEN TRUEBLOOD
Director, Student Ministry

KAREN DANIEL
Manager, Student Ministry Publishing

AMANDA MEJIAS
Production Leader

STEPHANIE CROSS
Content Editor

MORGAN HAWK
Production Editor

AMY LYON
Graphic Designer

EDITORIAL TEAM,
LIFEWAY WOMEN
BIBLE STUDIES

BECKY LOYD
Director, Lifeway Women

TINA BOESCH
Manager

CHELSEA WAACK
Production Leader

ELIZABETH HYNDMAN
Content Editor

TESSA MORRELL
Production Editor

LAUREN ERVIN
Art Director

SARAH HOBBS
Graphic Designer

TABLE OF CONTENTS

4 ABOUT THE AUTHOR

5 HOW TO USE THIS STUDY

6 SESSION ONE: Intro

14 SESSION TWO: Ashamed Isaiah

40 SESSION THREE: Ashamed at the Well

60 SESSION FOUR: Ashamed Peter

84 SESSION FIVE: Ashamed Paul

106 SESSION SIX: Shame Crucified

128 APPENDIX

135 ENDNOTES

136 LEADER & MOM GUIDES

138 ADDITIONAL RESOURCES

ABOUT THE AUTHOR

SCARLET HILTIBIDAL is the author of *Afraid of All the Things, You're the Worst Person in the World, He Numbered the Pores on My Face*, and the Bible study *Anxious*. She writes regular columns for *ParentLife* and *HomeLife Magazines* and devotionals for *She Reads Truth* and enjoys speaking to women around the country about the freedom and rest available in Jesus. Scarlet has a degree in biblical counseling and taught elementary school before she started writing. She and her husband live in Tennessee where she loves communicating in sign language with her three daughters, eating nachos by herself, writing for her friends, and studying stand-up comedy with a passion that should be reserved for more important pursuits.

HOW TO USE THIS STUDY

PERSONAL STUDY

Each week you'll have five days of personal study. Watch the video teaching after completing the five days of personal study. The first session is an introduction followed by the video teaching. If you're studying with a group, you can read the introduction together or on your own before you meet to watch the video and discuss.

VIDEO ACCESS

With the purchase of this book, you have access to videos from Scarlet that provide insight to help you better understand and apply what you study. You'll find detailed information on how to access the teaching videos in the back of your Bible study book.

GROUP TIME

Each session of *Ashamed* ends with a teaching video from Scarlet. The Watch page provides you with a place to take notes from the video teachings and from your small group discussion time. You'll want to begin your study by reading the Introduction, then watching the Session One video and taking notes on page 12.

LEADING A GROUP?

We've included a leader guide at the back of the book, which offers general tips and helps guide discussion. This study is also available for women, so you'll find a mom and daughter guide at the back of the book if you decide to do this study together.

1

INTRO

THEN SAID I, WOE
IS ME! FOR I AM
UNDONE; BECAUSE
I AM A MAN OF
UNCLEAN LIPS, AND
I DWELL IN THE
MIDST OF A PEOPLE
OF UNCLEAN LIPS:
FOR MINE EYES HAVE
SEEN THE KING, THE
LORD OF HOSTS.

ISAIAH 6:5, KJV

MEMORY VERSE

INTRODUCTION

We often hear or see affirmations from well-meaning people telling us we are worthy. "You are amazing! You are beautiful! You are worthy!" You can see the Instagram® post now, can't you? And I so want it to be true. I want to be worthy. I want to be worthy of love, of comfort, of success, of a day out with my best friends, of all the good stuff and none of the bad stuff, please. Don't you want that, too?

My first several years walking with Jesus were marked by a panicked desperation to obtain that worthiness. I thought being worthy would lead to comfort. It sounds so nice to be worthy. I still sometimes think that way.

Like, I may not be worthy in this moment, but I *could* be worthy if I tried hard enough, right?

At the moment I'm writing this, I'm on a plane, headed across the country to speak to a group of women about Jesus. Surely someone who writes for and speaks to women about Jesus and the Bible needs to be worthy, right? Especially by the time I stand on a platform and talk about the most important and definitely worthy Person who has ever lived.

Don't worry, friends. I'll get worthy by then. The conference isn't until tomorrow afternoon anyway. So, maybe not the end of this day, but surely worthiness will happen to me before tomorrow afternoon.

Here's the thing—it won't. We know that. Worthiness won't arrive just by me thinking about worthiness.

To think of myself as "worthy" is to forget the cross. It doesn't work. And every time I get caught up in a cycle of striving and failing, of focusing on what I do more than what Jesus does, I end up feeling temporary self-righteousness or devastated by shame. I so want to be worthy, but most often, what I feel is shame.

WHAT IS SHAME?

I think of shame as that horrible sinking feeling you get when you say the wrong thing, when you hurt someone you love, or when you realize you've done wrong and there's nothing you can do to fix it. That *if I could just get a redo of the last ten minutes* feeling. That feeling of, *Oh no, I've blown it. The thing or the person or the life I love is irreparably broken.*

We often feel shame because of things we've done, but we can find ourselves feeling ashamed for other reasons, too.

What about the girl who's struggling to find a date to the homecoming dance—or sits at home most Friday nights now that many of her friends have boyfriends? What about the girl who wishes she looked different or fit in with a different crowd? What about the girl who can't escape the gossip about her past?

I think of Elizabeth's story, which you can read in Luke 1. Elizabeth couldn't control her inability to conceive, and it made her feel shame. In these situations, shame may be cultural; it may not be the result of anything we've done but of circumstances beyond our control.

Or what about the shame you carry, not because of what you've done or not done, but because of what was done to you? Not the shame of your sin but the shame you carry because of how others have sinned against you.

You don't necessarily have to be the villain to feel like you are, right?

And there is also a deep and difficult kind of shame that comes from physical, emotional, or sexual abuse. We see a biblical example of this kind of shame in the life of Tamar (2 Sam. 13). If you've walked through this sort of trauma, we encourage you to find the support you need.*

Life is so hard. From the most extreme to the most "minor" situations, we have all felt humiliated, embarrassed, and ashamed. Shame is a sad reality in our broken world, especially for those of us who are in Christ. We weren't meant to live in hopelessness, crushed under the weight of shame.

HOPE FOR THE SHAMED

A long time ago, the prophet Isaiah stepped into the throne room of God, and he was "undone" by his brokenness in view of God's holiness. He cried out in despair, recognizing he shouldn't even be alive in the presence of such perfection. But then, a weird and beautiful thing happened—a terror-inducing angel, through the smoke and the shaking and the grandeur, touched Isaiah's mouth with a coal and told him his sin was forgiven. Isaiah's response? "HERE I AM. SEND ME. I DON'T CARE. I'M YOURS! I'LL DO WHATEVER!" That is the explosive beauty at the core of the Christian experience. Isaiah moved from death to life. He moved from being undone by shame to having hopeful humility and urgency to serve the Lord.

You guys, this is what Jesus does.

We were as good as dead, but the forgiveness of God gives us new life, new purpose, new confidence, new hope.

Unfortunately, many people never experience undoneness. They move through life convinced they are the source of greatness and hope. That doesn't work either. God designed our hearts to encounter their unworthiness, see God as glorious and gracious, and leave all self-sufficiency and shame behind as we trust in Him. Anything else leaves us hopelessly fighting to prove to ourselves and the world that we are worthy, when deep down we know no amount of effort can make us worthy.

> SO, WHAT ARE WE DOING HERE? WHY ARE YOU DOING THIS BIBLE STUDY? CIRCLE WHICH OF THE TWO FOLLOWING CATEGORIES YOU THINK YOU FALL INTO.

IF YOU'RE UNDONE (OR NEED TO BE)

If you're afraid you need to have your life together to participate in a Bible study, don't worry. It's actually the opposite. This is for undone people (and people who need to be undone). To be undone, like Isaiah, is to realize your unworthiness in the presence of the One who is worthy. The right amount of undoneness is good for us; it leads to humility and trust in God. I pray that this Bible study helps you see and remember that being undone in light of God's goodness is the right place to start.

IF YOU'RE TOO UNDONE

Maybe that's not you though. Maybe you feel a bit too undone. I think a lot of Christ followers get stuck in the undone place. Sometimes we catch a glimpse of the train of God's robe and the depth of our sin, and we feel crushed by how ridiculously we fall short. We fail to move on to the hopeful humility that flows from God's forgiveness.

If you've got the undone part down already, I want this Bible study to help you move beyond the shame of your sin to the joy-inducing, peace-producing thrill that comes from a lifestyle of repentance and a happy relationship with Jesus.

We were made to live in the light, confessing and repenting and renouncing our shame, because Jesus was shamed in our place. You can have that.

So, let's do this. Join me in Scripture for the next few weeks, and let's see the freedom available to us when we experience the mercy of God deeply. Let's study the Bible, do what it says, and enjoy what it gives.

I used to live life doing my best, hoping and straining for wholeness and peace and perfection. I wanted to move past my mistakes and never again do anything I regretted. I longed for the day when Jesus would come through the clouds and fix me so that I wouldn't break anything else. I worked, hoped, and longed, without realizing peace with God and joy in Jesus could exist for me today. Like, right now, in this very moment, before I take my next breath—I can be shame-free. I can rest. Because this day, this weekend, this life, is not about how well I'm able to perform; it's always only about how Jesus performed in my place.

When I remember the good news of the gospel of Jesus, I remember I don't have to be super perfect and polished; I can simply delight in the truth and power of God's Word. Shame is a lie. Jesus is better. Let's discover this together.

---

* Talk to your parents about finding a professional counselor in your area. You might want to check out websites like aacc.net, focusonthefamily.com/counseling, and biblicalcounseling.com, or ask your pastor or church leader for their recommendations. If you are currently in an abusive situation, please reach out to your local authorities or call the National Domestic Violence Hotline at 800.799.7233. There are people who can help you get to a place of safety.

SESSION 1 / GROUP TIME

WATCH

Write down any thoughts, verses, or things you want to remember as you watch the video for Session One.

_____

_____

_____

_____

_____

_____

_____

_____

_____

_____

_____

_____

_____

DISCUSS

Fear and shame make people run away and hide. That's sort of the exact opposite of going to a small group, so I hope you won't run. I want you to stay. Quickly, let's think about what we just saw in Genesis 3—Adam and Eve and the beginning of shame.

READ GENESIS 3:8-11 as a group. Keep in mind that this is after Adam and Eve, the first two created people, sinned against God by doing the one thing He had commanded them not to do. What did they do when they heard God coming?

To access the video teaching sessions, use the instructions in the back of your Bible study book.

In verse 10, what did Adam tell God he was feeling?

Adam was afraid because he felt exposed. Embarrassed, he wanted to run. Every single one of you, and everyone you know—and all of their families, friends, and classmates—knows this feeling well. When others see our shame, we want to hide. Don't feel like joining this group for six weeks is a commitment to spill your guts and compound your shame. The next six weeks are not about your past or exposing your guilt for all to see; they're about God and what He's done to free you from it. Stay, focus on Him, and share what you feel comfortable sharing. The more this group helps you see the power and love of God, the more you will want to run to Him, not run and hide.

Get to know your group! Share names, which school you go to, and what you like to do for fun.

What's your first memory of a moment of shame or embarrassment?

Do you feel like you've had an "undone" moment, like Isaiah? If so, share what it was like when you saw your need for God.

Have you ever felt stuck in your shame? What are some unhelpful (or only temporarily helpful) things you've turned to in those moments that didn't end up helping the way you hoped they would?

What hopes do you have in your personal walk with God as you start this study?

PRAY

Come before God together and ask that He help each of you understand His grace more deeply as you study and to extend that grace to one another.

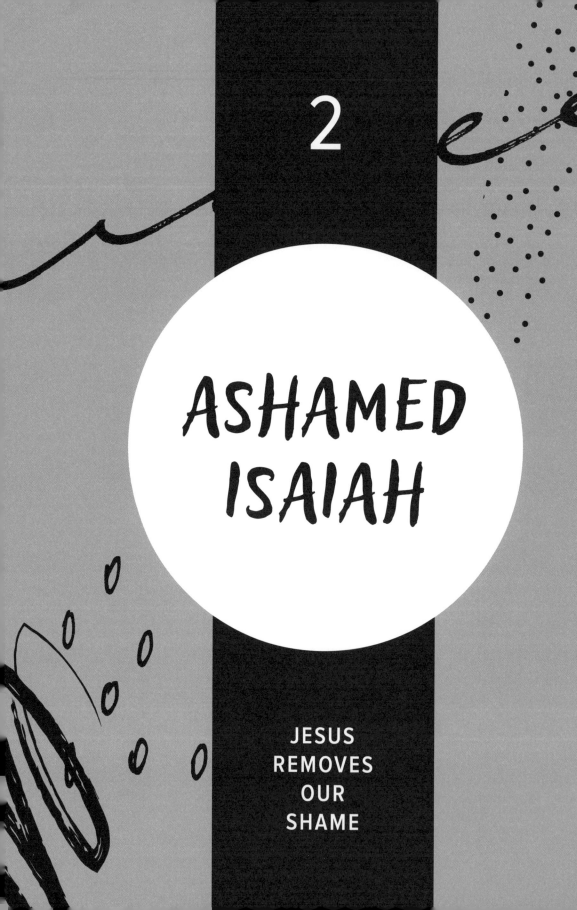

2

ASHAMED ISAIAH

JESUS
REMOVES
OUR
SHAME

HE TOUCHED MY
MOUTH WITH IT AND
SAID: NOW THAT THIS
HAS TOUCHED YOUR
LIPS, YOUR INIQUITY
IS REMOVED AND YOUR
SIN IS ATONED FOR.
THEN I HEARD THE
VOICE OF THE LORD
ASKING: WHO WILL
I SEND? WHO WILL GO
FOR US? I SAID: HERE
I AM. SEND ME.

ISAIAH 6:7-8

MEMORY VERSE

ASPIRING WITNESS PROTECTION PARTICIPANT

ISAIAH 6

Every time I experience any conflict of any kind, I want to move to a new city. I love getting away from problems. I have often wondered what it would be like to join the Witness Protection Program. Not because of any personal danger—I can't recall witnessing any substantive crimes. I just rrreaalllly like fresh starts.

I've been fresh-starting like it was my job since I was born, before I even had a say in it. By the age of five, I'd already lived in Los Angeles, New York City, Connecticut, and Miami. Since then, I've lived in Nashville and Orange County, and now Nashville again.

You probably don't have much control over where you live or how often your family moves, but maybe you know the feeling of wanting a fresh start. Maybe you've wanted to change schools or go to a different church. Maybe you constantly change your hair color or try new things or flit from one group of friends to another. Maybe you lose yourself in books, movies, or social media where you get to be absorbed into a new story.

Those things aren't necessarily wrong, but maybe, like me, you've been informally and accidentally witness-protectioning yourself for a long time.

I think I've sometimes been running from shame. I seem to lean toward running and hiding rather than staying and serving because I don't want to feel the shame of my brokenness or weakness. I don't want to be confronted with the fact that I am human and imperfect and sinful. It sounds awful, you know?

> While you probably don't have any say over where you live, can you relate? What is your typical response to conflict?

If you tend to run from shame, where do you usually run or hide? Circle anything that hits you, then explain why you run or hide this way.

SCROLLING
SOCIAL MEDIA   WATCHING A MOVIE   SWITCHING GROUPS
                                                 OF FRIENDS OFTEN

                    ALWAYS   BINGING A
PURSUING   KEEPING BUSY   TV SHOW
PERFECT GRADES
                                            CHANGING YOUR STYLE
                                            OR APPEARANCE
    READING A NOVEL   OTHER

But God does incredible, miraculous, shame-crushing, joy-inducing things when we admit and confess our sin. One of the most beautiful examples of this is in the book of Isaiah.

READ ISAIAH 6. Then look back at verses 1-5, and list five things Isaiah witnessed in those verses.

1.

2.

3.

4.

5.

Write out the phrase the seraphim shouted to each other.

What a scene. It sounds terrifying, overwhelming, otherworldly—*kind of weird, actually*—right?

Isaiah's iniquity—a big word for sin—was removed. The book of Isaiah was originally written in Hebrew, and the words *your iniquity* are translated from a word that means, *guilt, punishment for iniquity.*[1]

So, not only was Isaiah relieved of the punishment he deserved, but he was also relieved of the guilt. That's huge. Consider that again—God doesn't just remove the punishment; He removes the guilt. We've all felt guilt before, so we know guilt is a too-heavy-to-carry punishment in itself.

Just like that—*poof*—guilt is removed. Have you ever faced trouble and gotten away with it?

Picture that situation in your mind. Maybe your parents still don't know about that lie or that night or that mistake to this day. Maybe you carried shame for a while but eventually got over it. Or maybe you're still not over it.

Here, with the angels and God and Isaiah, we see a man who was thoroughly guilty standing before the God who sees all and knows all. And instead of destroying him, God forgave him. It's hard to even imagine what that must be like, right?

READ ISAIAH 6:8-13, and answer the following questions.

What did God ask?

How did Isaiah answer?

What mission did God have for Isaiah?

That mission sounds pretty horrible. God sent Isaiah out to deliver bad news from God. He told Isaiah how it was going to work out, and how it worked out was not great.

Has God ever called you to something that felt pretty horrible? Explain.

If you did what God called you to, how did it work out for you and the people around you?

In those early figuring-it-out years of my faith, I wouldn't have had much to write in spaces like the one above. My fear and shame kept me from obedience. My fear and shame kept me from living for God, listening to God, and being blessed by taking part in the mission of God.

But the more I began to understand my own sinfulness and just how much it took for God to redeem me—just how much love and mercy was involved— the easier it was to take baby steps in the direction He led. As soon as I started taking those steps, the blessings He poured out on me and the people around me were overwhelming.

Blessings like purpose, peace, and joy.

Do fear and shame keep you from walking in obedience? If so, what does that look like in your life?

If you answered yes to that last question, remember what Isaiah's coal-meets-lips scenario means for you. Like Isaiah, we are unworthy when faced with the purity of our perfect, all-powerful God. But that hot coal reminds us God is so loving that He offers us forgiveness. While Isaiah's forgiveness was symbolized with a burning coal, our forgiveness is offered through the sacrificial death and resurrection of Jesus Christ.

> What baby step can you take as you seek to live the mission God is calling you to? How can you say, "Here I am; send me," this week?

I think Andrew Davis sums this up powerfully. In *Exalting Jesus in Isaiah*, he writes:

> *What a beautiful sequence in this narrative: a vision of the enthroned Lord in his glory leads to overpowering heavenly worship, and it also leads to Isaiah's awareness of his sinfulness, which leads to him crying out against himself, which leads to the atoning work for his sin, which leads to hearing the Lord call for a messenger, which leads to Isaiah presenting himself for service. In this sense, Isaiah 6 stands as a lasting paradigm for all who would enter the Lord's service.*[2]

In short, awareness and repentance of sin leads us to offer ourselves up to the Lord for His work.

Close out this day meditating on this beautiful paradigm and praying that the Lord will help your mind release the shame of your mistakes, that He'll help you remember His Son's payment for your sins, that He'll help you renounce your fear of the future, and that you'll feel His nearness as you do something eternal today.

COWERING FROM CONSECRATED COUSINS

LUKE 14:7-14, 25-33; ISAIAH 6:7

The times I've felt most ashamed were the same times I witnessed someone else's apparent act of kindness or sacrifice. Someone else's "Here I am; send me" moments often point out my lack of them.

I will never forget running into some distant cousins at a family function and avoiding them like I avoided germs in 2020. Note: They are lovely cousins, but they were fresh off the plane from two international adoptions for a couple of sweetheart girls with special needs.

How wonderful, beautiful, and noble, right?

Well, instead of asking questions or encouraging them, I had this weirdly timed urge to stand in the bathroom and check my hair every time they came near.

In my mind, the adoption-loving cousins were in the throne room with the shouting seraphim, and I was unworthy and unwilling—the opposite of all the good things they were.

Their selflessness shined a spotlight on how selfishly I was living.

Their courage reminded me of how comfortable I'd become hiding from my purpose in the world.

Enter the restroom. Check hair. Feel shame. Repeat.

Their evident fruit reminded me of how fruitless my life looked. And I didn't like it.

Woe is me! I am unworthy of having small talk with these superhero humans, and I'm not sure I want to do what it seems to take to be worthy.

Though my comfort-craving heart lies to me and tells me that a good life is an easy one, God has never skirted around the reality of His holiness or the very real cost of following Him.

Can you think of a time in your life when being around holiness or goodness shined a light on your guilt and made you want to run away? Reflect on that in the space provided.

READ LUKE 14:7-14.

In this passage of Scripture, Jesus was eating at the house of one of the leading Pharisees, a religious leader of the time. After observing their behavior, He taught them about humility.

How would you define *humility*?

How is humility demonstrated in this example from Jesus?

The Bible talks about humility a lot. We must humble ourselves to know God. We must humble ourselves to recognize our need for Him in the first place.

READ LUKE 14:25-33. What is the cost of following Jesus?

The cost of following Christ is great. We must be willing to bear our own crosses—ready to give up everything to follow Him. This is including, but not limited to, giving up our pride. When we recognize our need for Jesus, when we realize we can't save ourselves or earn holiness, when we understand we will never be worthy on our own, that is humbling.

It might even sound humiliating. Well, one of the coolest things I ever learned was how different "humility" and "humiliation" are.

Here are some synonyms for the word *humiliate*: dishonor, disgrace, mortify, shame, degrade, take down, cheapen.

On the contrary, here's a list of synonyms for *humility*: modesty, meekness, lack of pride, lowliness, down-to-earthness.

Those are pretty different lists for two words that sound so similar and are so often mixed up.

One word suggests a sort of self-loathing, and the other looks a lot like Jesus.

Do you struggle with viewing these two words as equals? Do you feel holier when you are beating yourself up? Take a minute to write out what this struggle looks like (or has looked like in the past) for you.

In the table below, write down what God's Word says about true biblical humility.

SCRIPTURE	WHAT WE LEARN ABOUT HUMILITY
Micah 6:8	
Proverbs 18:12	
Isaiah 57:15	
1 Peter 5:5	

Whew. The Bible has a lot to say about humility, doesn't it? And that list is nowhere near exhaustive. Looking over all this Scripture, I noticed how frequently God's people are commanded to be humble.

Commands like these can be difficult to wrap your mind around, because with any fruit of the Spirit or Christlike way of being, if you pursue said good thing for the wrong reasons, you never find it. Like, if I say to myself, *I want to be humble so that I am awesome and loved by God and people,* I'm doing it wrong.

LOOK BACK AT ISAIAH 6:7. What caused Isaiah's humility?

Forgiveness! Isaiah's experience and awareness of the undeserved and dramatic forgiveness he received from the holy, perfect, true God humbled him.

As you close out this day, ask the Holy Spirit to help you identify where you might be stuck in humiliation. Ask Him to help your heart move toward humility.

A SWEET, SHAMELESS REDHEAD
ISAIAH 50; LUKE 7:36-50; PSALM 103:11-14

Isaiah 50 is about listening to God—even when it means suffering. After His encounter with God in chapter 6, Isaiah was a willing prophet who obediently delivered tons of bad news about God's coming judgment. Isaiah listened and obeyed. Good job, Isaiah! But remember, Isaiah was also "a man of unclean lips" (6:5). Isaiah was a sinner.

Other than being the bearer of bad news, Isaiah is known for prophesying about the coming Messiah. If you're new to Christianity and you don't know what any of those words mean, here, *prophesying* means foretelling the future. *Messiah* means Savior. Yes, Isaiah was telling the nation of Judah a whole lot about God's coming judgment. But Isaiah was also sharing the ground-breaking, globe-shaking news that God, in His mercy, would send a Savior. Jesus, the One who would, quoting the *Lord of the Rings* series here, "make everything sad come untrue."[3]

And here, in Isaiah 50, we get to hear more from Isaiah—a sometimes obedient but flawed and imperfect servant—writing about the coming of a perfectly obedient, perfectly unselfish Servant. He was writing about Jesus before Jesus came.

LOOK UP ISAIAH 50, AND READ VERSES 4-10 from the perspective of the perfectly obedient Servant to come (Jesus). What does verse 4 say God had given Him?

What did Jesus say He did not do in verse 5?

What future thing does it sound like Jesus was describing in verse 6? (Hint: read John 19.)

I want you to pay such special attention to Isaiah 50:7. So, go ahead and copy it down in the space provided.

In this verse, we can see the nature of Jesus displayed—He is one hundred percent man, but He is also one hundred percent God. The math doesn't add up, but it's true. He is the Son of God, and God sent Him to live a sinless life on earth, to die on the cross for our sins, and to be raised again, defeating death.

For most of us, the events described by Isaiah in verse 6 would be humiliating. To be beaten and mocked and spit on? Sounds like the worst, right?

But verse 7 tells us Jesus would not be humiliated. Why? Because He is God, and He knows the end. He knows the results will not be humiliation but vindication.

Because of this heaven-touching-earth moment, we can echo our Savior and say, "I have not been humiliated . . . I will not be put to shame." That is true for us in Jesus. Hallelujah.

So, what can our lives look like when we remember and embrace this reality?

Before I'd spent much time with Jesus or much time in His Word, I worked at a church. I remember the sweet redhead who worked at the front desk just exploding with love and happiness. She was truly the quintessential front desk person. She made everyone who came to her feel completely wrapped in care and kindness. I remember commenting on it one day and she said, "Oh, the one who's been forgiven much loves much!"

How brilliant! I thought, not realizing that she was literally quoting Jesus.

READ LUKE 7:36-50. How did the woman in this story behave around Jesus, and what did the Pharisees think about it?

In verses 44-47, Jesus explained why her behavior was appropriate and beautiful. Put His explanation into your own words.

Who have you met who seemed to be genuinely humble? Describe how that person lived and how he or she made you feel.

What a beautiful thing that the Spirit of God in the lives of believers leads to humility. But even people who look a lot like Jesus will let us down in this life. Thankfully, we can study the life of Jesus, and in Him, we see and know and hear from the only One who perfectly humbled Himself (Phil. 2:8) even though He had every reason not to.

In seasons when I've suffered with depression or grief or anxiety, when I've spent hours awake in the middle of the night cycling through the worst moments on my "shame reel" (more on the shame reel later), the thought of being someone like Sweet Redhead feels impossible.

In the space below, quickly jot down the mindsets or negative thoughts you carry with you.

READ PSALM 103:11-14. What point did the psalmist make about our sins (or transgressions)?

What did he make about God?

Okay, spend more time on this part please. ◡̈

Go back over the list you wrote on the previous page of your negative thoughts and scribble out those things with passion and pressure like your life depends on it, so you can't make out a single word you wrote.

Jesus is better and stronger than anything you can ever write. He gives His best and His strength to you. Because of Jesus's sacrifice, our compassionate God has removed our transgressions "as far as the east is from the west" (Ps. 103:12).

Now, close this day and take all the time you need to write down as many things as you can think of that remind you of the goodness of God. When you are tempted to replay your shame reel or tell yourself lies about who God is and who you are, remember what the Bible says—our God is good and compassionate. Use the following verses to jog your memory and write down ways you've noticed this goodness in your life.

- Exodus 34:6

- Psalm 23

- Psalm 145:8-10

- John 3:15-18

- Philippians 1:6

- James 1:17

BROKEN THINGS AND DEBTS TO PAY

ISAIAH 53:1-12

When I was a poor newlywed, my husband and I shared a car. I often had to carpool or wait for rides. One day, the kindergarten teacher at my school noticed my plight and said, "I have an extra car sitting in my garage that's not being driven. My husband and I want to loan it to you."

What a gift! I was so grateful. But almost immediately, car-borrowing-tragedy struck. The loaner was an older convertible and one day, I rolled down the window to find that it wouldn't roll back up. When it started to rain and a few droplets threatened the interior leather of my borrowed car, I panicked. I ran inside and found black trash bags and duct tape (things you always keep on hand when you're broke), and I duct taped the sweet kindergarten teacher's car up.

I felt horrified and humiliated having to tell her that I broke her car. In an act of sheer mercy, she said, "Scarlet, don't worry about it. We will fix the window. Just leave it in the parking lot."

Humiliating, yes. Relieving? So much yes.

Have you ever had someone take the fall for you? What happened?

When have you broken something you borrowed, and the person told you not to worry about it?

Fast-forward a decade, and we had enough extra income to buy an iPad® but not enough to replace it if something were to happen. So, when someone from our church borrowed the iPad and returned it broken, I found it easy to say, "Don't worry about it." Not because we had money to replace it, but because people had done the same for us. God had done the same for us.

When you know how it feels to have a debt paid for you, it's a joy to do the same for others.

It should work the same way for us as followers of Christ.

> When has a friend borrowed something from you and given it back broken or in worse condition than when she borrowed it? How did you respond?

We can have the joy of living out each day we're given in light of this overwhelming debt Christ has paid for us. We can be the most gracious people in the world because we know what it is to be ashamed and humiliated and panicked because we've broken something and don't have the means to fix it.

> How would you respond differently in a similar situation, considering how Jesus has paid the greatest debt you owed?

READ ISAIAH 53:1-12. Who is this "guilt offering" Isaiah wrote about, and what does this passage tell you about Him?

The detail we are given about Jesus hundreds of years before His birth amazes me. God's people were told what He'd be like, how He'd arrive, and about the shame He would carry.

LOOK BACK AT ISAIAH 53. What does verse 6 say about us?

How did God respond to our actions, according to that verse?

Now, look up the following verses, and write down what they say about our debt.

SCRIPTURE	WHAT WE LEARN ABOUT DEBT
Romans 6:23	
Ephesians 1:7	
Hebrews 7:27	
1 Peter 1:18-19	
1 Peter 2:24	
1 John 2:1-2	

We are so indebted to our Creator and Rescuer, it would break our brains to fully grasp it.

Our shame often comes from going our own way rather than looking for God's way. But verse 6 shows us that He did make a way for our debt to be paid: He laid all our shame over every sin in our past, present, and future on His Son's capable shoulders. For every time we go our own way, there is grace because of Jesus.

I get it—God's way isn't always easy to see. And when we do see God's way, it's not always easy to follow or stick to it.

Think about a situation where you need to choose how to move forward. Write out what it would look like to go your own way, then read the following verses and go back and describe what it might look like to go God's way instead.

• Situation:

• Going my own way:

• Going God's way:

• What God's Word says: Matthew 5:1-12; 6:26-34; Luke 6:27-28; Romans 12:18; Galatians 5:22-23; 2 Timothy 1:7; 1 Peter 5:7

Read 1 John 1:9. What can you do if you've already chosen your own way?

Read John 14:26 and Acts 1:8. How can you choose differently in the future?

Spend a few moments praying, thanking God for sending His Son to die in your place. Thank Him for His forgiveness and love.

ISAIAH ALL OVER THE PLACE
ISAIAH 61:1-2; LUKE 4:16-19; JOHN 12:37-41

The book of Isaiah is the most frequently quoted book elsewhere in the Bible. Why? Why is it so important that other biblical authors kept sharing it? What about Isaiah is so fundamental to our faith?

Put simply, Isaiah kept saying Jesus was coming. Girls, Isaiah clearly presented the message of the gospel seven hundred years before the gospel was fulfilled. He predicted it in great detail—accurately.

Think about a movie or book where a character has quite the reputation for protecting those they love—they will go to any lengths to keep their people safe. What book or movie comes to mind? Why?

Does it seem believable to you—characters who will do absolutely anything for the good of the people they love? Why or why not?

Sometimes these kinds of sentiments and relationships just seem too good to be true. If that's the case for us today, can you even imagine how this would have sounded to the hearers of Isaiah's words back in those pre-Rescuer days?

All this to say, the book of Isaiah is important because it pointed to the reality of the Rescuer who was to come. And then He came, and He and the people around Him were like, "Remember what Isaiah said? Open your eyes!"

OPEN UP TO JOHN 12:37-41. In my Bible, there's a subheading that says, "Isaiah's Prophecies Fulfilled." Read through the verses, and in the space below, list the verses from Isaiah referenced in this passage in John. (Hint: look at the footnotes or cross references in your Bible.)

Rewrite the prophecies from Isaiah in your own words.

Here in John, we see Jesus living out the calling that Isaiah prophesied about in real time.

READ LUKE 4:16-19. What town was Jesus in, and what did He read from?

What Jesus read there in His hometown was not random at all.

READ ISAIAH 61:1-2. Which specific phrases do you see here that you just read in the Gospel of Luke?

Isn't that incredible? And it's just one of many examples of this. Jesus was the long-awaited hope, the way-better-than-any-character Hero. He didn't provide us temporary safety; He bled and died and rose again, giving eternal hope to our broken hearts.

Raise your hand if you forgot you were doing a Bible study about shame? Looking at intricate fulfillments of this hope makes it difficult to think about lesser things—even our shame. And that's the whole point.

God is so wonderful, so compassionate, so loving. He overwhelms lesser things in our lives and gives us what we need. He has given us signs and wonders and details and miracles—as if salvation wasn't enough! We can look through this alive and active book (Heb. 4:12) and see His provision and His hand, throughout history, on every page. Why do we so often doubt His hand in our own lives?

This may look a little daunting, but it's going to be really cool. On the left, you'll see a New Testament reference and what the reference points to. As you read these passages, look closely at the little letters, numbers, and footnotes. In each of these verses, you can see which verse of prophecy it is fulfilling and where it's found in Isaiah. I've done the first couple for you.

MATTHEW 1:23 A virgin will become pregnant	*Isaiah 7:14*
MATTHEW 12:21 Jesus is hope for the Gentiles	*Isaiah 42:1-4*
MARK 9:48 What eternal separation from God is like ("Fire is not quenched . . . ")	
LUKE 4:17-19 Jesus is anointed to preach	
JOHN 12:39-40 Blinded eyes and hardened hearts	
ACTS 8:32-33 Jesus led like a sheep to the slaughter	
ROMANS 9:33 Believers will not be disappointed	
1 CORINTHIANS 15:54-56 Death swallowed up	

Jesus is good news. The gospel is good news. Death has been "swallowed up in victory" (1 Cor. 15:54). Your shame from failures—past, present, and future—shrivel up in that kind of hope, right? Believe this promise. Memorize it. Cling to it. Jesus has swallowed up our shame and given us the victory. We can have true and lasting peace.

SESSION 2 / GROUP TIME

WATCH

Write down any thoughts, verses, or things you want to remember as you watch the video for Session Two.

To access the video teaching sessions, use the instructions in the back of your Bible study book.

DISCUSS

On Day One, we read about when Isaiah was forgiven in the throne room of God. Have you ever experienced awe and undoneness over the holiness of God? How so?

This session's main idea is "Jesus removes our shame." If you are open to sharing, tell your group a brief testimony of shame you carried and how the Lord is helping you release it.

In the chart you filled out on Day Four (p. 32), which verse about debt was most meaningful to you? Why?

What is one new habit you can add to your life to help you fight shame with God's Word?

HE TOUCHED MY MOUTH WITH IT AND SAID: NOW THAT THIS HAS TOUCHED YOUR LIPS, YOUR INIQUITY IS REMOVED AND YOUR SIN IS ATONED FOR. THEN I HEARD THE VOICE OF THE LORD ASKING: WHO WILL I SEND? WHO WILL GO FOR US? I SAID: HERE I AM. SEND ME.

ISAIAH 6:7-8

PRAY

Thank God for sending Jesus to make a way for sinful people to be near to a holy God. Spend the remainder of your time in prayer. Pray specifically that God would help you and each member of your group fight feelings of shame and guilt by filling your minds with the truth of His Word.

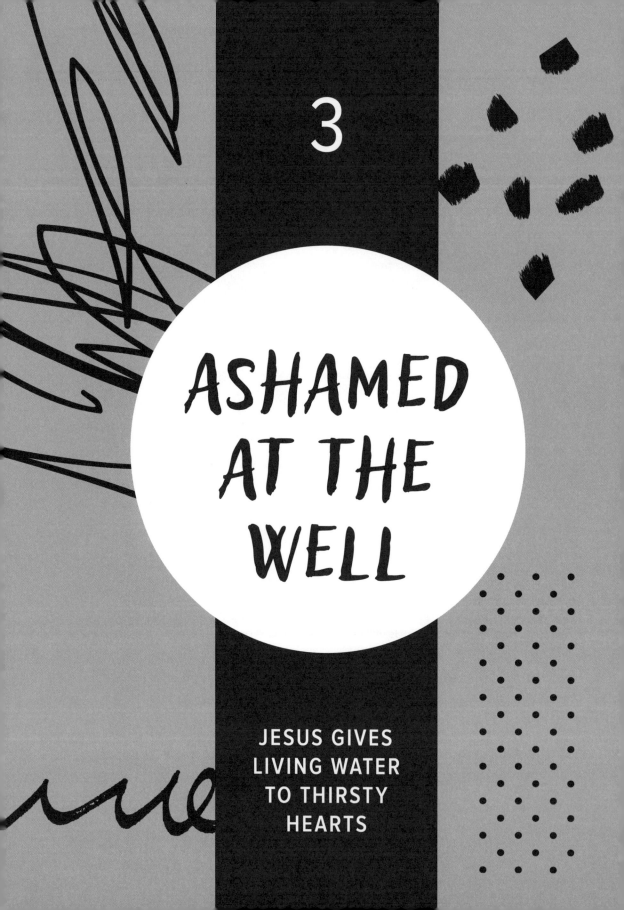

3

ASHAMED AT THE WELL

JESUS GIVES LIVING WATER TO THIRSTY HEARTS

JESUS SAID, "EVERYONE WHO DRINKS FROM THIS WATER WILL GET THIRSTY AGAIN. BUT WHOEVER DRINKS FROM THE WATER THAT I WILL GIVE HIM WILL NEVER GET THIRSTY AGAIN. IN FACT, THE WATER I WILL GIVE HIM WILL BECOME A WELL OF WATER SPRINGING UP IN HIM FOR ETERNAL LIFE."

JOHN 4:13-14

MEMORY VERSE

TOO GOOD TO BE TRUE?

JOHN 4:1-14; 7:37-38; 10:10

Have you ever been shocked by someone's kindness? I grew up in big cities—you walk fast, do your thing, and watch out for yourself. But I'll never forget my first day in Nashville when a man in a parking lot said, "Hey!," and I jumped in fear, assuming I was about to die. But he wasn't a murderer or a mugger. He was just saying hello.

Experiencing such a gracious culture was weird and striking. But southern hospitality isn't a huge deal compared to the text we're about to look at.

Today's story isn't "city girl meets southerners." Jews and Samaritans were not just slightly culturally different—they didn't mix at all. They hated each other.

Samaria had been captured by the Assyrians, who deported many of the Jews, settling with and marrying remaining Jews and practicing their religion their way. So, Jewish people looked down on Samaritans politically, religiously, and racially. D. A. Carson explains that the Jews "viewed the Samaritans not only as the children of political rebels, but as racial half-breeds whose religion was tainted by various unacceptable elements."[1]

Their beef also included a disagreement about where they believed God's people should worship.

The conflict was so intense by the time Jesus was around that Jews wouldn't even pass through Samaria when they traveled. They'd cross the Jordan River instead. This wasn't bumping into a frenemy at the grocery store—this was Capulet and Montague level tension.

Before Jesus even opened His mouth, the woman in today's passage likely felt a unique sort of cultural shame just at the sight of a Jewish man at a Samaritan well. So, when Jesus spoke to the woman at the well, it wasn't just a friendly Nashville wave hello. It was a radical, beautiful, cross-cultural, theological statement.

What kinds of cultural shame exist in our world today?

READ JOHN 4:1-14. Why did Jesus stop in Samaria when He was traveling through?

What did He ask of the Samaritan woman? How did she react?

Have you ever questioned someone's kindness as too good to be true? Like when your friend hurts you and then tells you that you look pretty today? Or when you want to go out with your friends, so you compliment your parents?

Think of a time when you've questioned someone's motives. Jot down a few of the details.

Were you right or wrong? Explain.

The Samaritan woman knew it didn't make sense for a Jew to stop by for some water, so she questioned Him. What was this guy's angle?

What did Jesus tell her He could offer her in verse 10?

How did she show she didn't understand what He meant?

I'm going to be honest with you—if I didn't already know this story, I'd question the phrase "living water" too. What does that mean? I picture some sort of sci-fi water creature made with special effects. But Jesus often used words with double meanings. Later in the Gospel, He explained a little more.

READ JOHN 7:37-38. What is the living water in this passage?

"If you knew," Jesus said, "you would ask him" (4:10). That is such a powerful statement. Not just for the woman at the well, who clearly didn't know who she was talking to, but for girls who walk around with shame, forgetting we have all-the-time access to the One who died to take that shame away. "If you only knew . . . "

FLIP FORWARD A FEW PAGES TO JOHN 10:10. Why did Jesus come to earth?

If we know Christ, we should ask Him for help when we feel ashamed. We ask even if we are ashamed because of religious, cultural, or racial tension like the Samaritan woman. These things feel too big to tackle, but just like Jesus walked right into Samaria and spoke straight to that woman, He walked right into our broken world and offered us an abundant life.

When have you felt shame over something you thought was too big for Jesus to tackle? How is He speaking straight to your heart through today's Scripture?

The living water is available if we will drink, no matter the severity of the source of our shame. Shame is washed away when we know Jesus. When we ask, He gives living water.

What shame are you still holding onto that you need to hand over to Jesus? What would it take for you to let go of your shame and take hold of the abundant life He offers?

Today, pray about and around the sort of shame you or people you interact with might experience, not based on sin but based on outside expectations. Pray that you and those you serve will experience healing and renewed confidence—the kind that comes from the Lord.

DAY TWO

RECOGNIZED AT THE REGISTER

JOHN 4:11-26

I had an unusual childhood. You don't recognize you lived an unusual childhood until you're older and enough people say, "That's not normal." My mom was a TV and movie star, and my biological dad was a magician/fire-eater. What a sentence. But it was totally normal to me.

Everywhere we went, no matter the city or store, people freaked out and asked my mom for her autograph—the whole thing. My mom has a very distinct voice, and people would often say things like, "You sound JUST LIKE that girl from *Saturday Night Live*." Yep, there's a reason for that.

I remember her sweetly smiling and saying, "I'm her," but sometimes they refused to believe it. I'd seen enough people freak out over meeting her, that I remember thinking, "These people have no idea who they're talking to! If they believed her, this would be a highlight of their year, and they'd talk about it forever!"

Jesus wasn't a sparkly TV star, but word of His miraculous healings and His fulfillment of prophecy was spreading. People who recognized who He really was walked away with changed lives. But many people didn't believe. Many people didn't know. They walked away not recognizing the significance of the Person they'd met.

At first, the woman at the well clearly didn't understand who she was talking to either.

> **READ JOHN 4:11-26.** What questions did the woman ask Jesus in verses 11-12?

I love this. I love how her questions reveal her lack of understanding, and I love how Jesus responded, not with an answer to her question, but with what she needed to actually understand.

I can think back on so many times I've prayed, asking God questions about details and specifics—temporary things—and He has answered me by lifting my eyes upward, by expanding my view, and by reminding me of who He is and what is eternal.

Write briefly about a time in your life you did not understand.

How would your feelings have changed if you had been reminded of who God is—faithful, good, compassionate, sovereign—in your moment of confusion?

Today's passage is a comfort for those of us who open our Bibles and don't always understand what we're reading. We might be trying to find answers or fixes. Sometimes we might read for answers to questions like, "God, how do I stop letting the gossip hurt me and be confident in who You've made me to be?" Or "God, how long do I have to wait for the acceptance letter to my top school?" Or "God, when will I get to have a relationship-goals kind of boyfriend?" And instead of Magic 8 Ball® answers, we're met with Jesus. Instead of logistics, we find love, comfort, and peace in the living, active Word.

Do you ever ask God questions or look to His Word for the wrong reasons? What does that look like for you?

LOOK BACK AT VERSES 13-14. What does the living water Jesus offers do for people?

"Eternal life" can sound like a weird phrase, and we sometimes become desensitized to it, but it is the ultimate good thing. The absence of death, disease, and pain. The presence of God, glory, and perfection. Never ending.

That's what Jesus offered the Samaritan woman. It wasn't an extra special seltzer water—it was forever and abundant life.

So, where does shame come into play in this story? Let's take a look.

REREAD VERSES 15-26.

Notice how Jesus chose to reveal Himself to this woman. He could have told her about the living water, seen her lack of understanding, and went on His way. But He revealed Himself as more than an unlikely conversation partner by telling her about the shameful things He knew she'd done and was doing, things He shouldn't and couldn't have known about.

How did the woman respond? Who did she think Jesus was at first?

How would you react if someone showed up and lovingly but honestly addressed your shame, then showed you a better way?

In verse 26, Jesus was clearer than clear about who He is. He identified Himself as the long-awaited Messiah. Here, our well woman had an opportunity to either believe Jesus was who He said He was and walk away changed or be like those people with my mom—"You might sound like her, but you're not her. Next."

> *Jesus offered the woman a chance to believe, and in believing, a chance at freedom from shame. She was a shame-filled woman. He was a shame-lifting Savior. And in one well-side moment, Jesus offered her the abundant life she could never find on her own.*

BEFORE AND AFTER

JOHN 4:27-42

It's such an amazing, beautiful, shame-slaying thing when people share their stories. The woman at the well had a lot to say in the "before" part of her story. But today, we get to see how God redeemed her "before" for a beautiful "after"—not just for her but for everyone around her too.

What adjectives would you use to describe the Samaritan woman's "before"?

How would you describe your before?

READ JOHN 4:27-42. How would you describe the Samaritan woman's "after"?

How would you describe your after?

Jesus told her He had living water. Then, when His disciples told Him to eat, He spoke of food.

What was Jesus communicating through His figurative use of food and water?

I'm currently obsessed with Chipotle® bowls and Arnold Palmers® (which is iced tea and lemonade). I don't know your go-tos, but I know you have them, because our core needs as human beings are food and drink. Without them, our bodies die. A relationship with God through Jesus is like that but on a forever level. If our bodies don't have food and water, they die. If our souls don't have Jesus, we are just marking days and walking hopelessly toward the end. We were made for Him, so there is no true life in His absence.

Do you think someone looking at your life would know Jesus is necessary for your survival? Why or why not?

What can you do to show more clearly that Jesus is the reason for your hope?

Reading about the Samaritan woman is so encouraging, because shame-wise, she had so much going against her. She was carrying her shame for reasons that were her fault and reasons that were outside of her control. But after this encounter with Jesus, everything changed.

This woman's testimony was brief. Read it again in verse 39. What did she say? How did people react?

What about the woman's story do you think made the people want to find Jesus and learn more?

Verse 39 tells us many Samaritans believed because of her testimony, but others needed more. They went to Jesus Himself and then believed because of their own encounters with Him. Isn't that incredible? It's so true for all of us who follow Jesus. If we share our stories of how the Messiah moved us from shame and slavery and hopelessness to abundant life, we will get to see lives changed, for sure. But that story-sharing mainly points people to Jesus and leads them to their own encounters with Him.

If you are a believer, how would you describe your encounter with Jesus in one line, like the woman at the well?

Have you ever gotten to lead someone to Jesus by sharing your story? Or have you ever heard someone else's story of her encounter with Jesus and been moved? What was it about her story that drew you in?

Write more about it below, and finish out this day by thanking Jesus for allowing us to help people walk away from shame and toward life in Him.

THE CYCLE OF SELF-CARE
JOHN 7:37-39

At this point, Jesus's ministry was still not public, but word about Him was spreading. The beginning of chapter 7 tells us Jesus was traveling in Galilee because the Jewish religious people in Judea were trying to kill Him. To the Jewish people who made their whole lives about following God's law, Jesus was a blasphemer, a threat to the system, and Someone who acted as though He were God Himself—and the truth is, He is.

So, in this part of chapter 7, we see Jesus teaching at a festival. If you look back at the Old Testament laws, Jewish men were required to go to a number of feasts every year (Deut. 16). Based on the timeline, historians think the celebration Jesus attended in John 7 was the Festival of Shelters (aka the Festival of Tabernacles or Feast of Booths). The event lasted seven days (Lev. 23:34), and it was a time when Jewish people celebrated that God had brought the Israelites through the wilderness. So, Galilee would have been busy at this time of year. Lots of people around. Plenty of partying. But Jesus came secretly, still not broadcasting His presence because His time had "not yet arrived" (John 7:6).

> **READ JOHN 7:37-39.** What need did the people have that Jesus identified here?

Thirst for water is a universal need. Remember how crazy 2020 was, seeing everyone scared and suffering over the same thing? Thirst. Need. We all have it. We all know what longing feels like. We all know what it is to want something, to desire the always-fleeting and ever-elusive feeling of being fulfilled. It's cool to me that Jesus spoke to people in a way that immediately cut through whatever social or cultural filters they had. Just like the woman at the well, people knew the comfort and provision they could find on their own wouldn't last forever.

What or who do you usually look to for comfort? What or who has been your go-to lately? Why?

Do you see your comfort-seeking as a desire to mask shame? How so?

Experts will tell you "positive self talk" and "self-care" is the answer to fighting your shame. But try those things for a while, and you'll end up returning to the well again and again, longing for a deeper healing, for a comfort and satisfaction that goes the distance. You were made to hear another voice. You were made for a deeper care. And your Father wants you to have it.

What did Jesus tell the people in Galilee to do to quench their thirst?

What was He referring to when He promised streams of living water (v. 39)?

For the hearers of those words in Galilee, Jesus promised His Spirit to come. The God who made us promised to live in us. He promised eternal healing from sin and the shame it brings.

As Jesus's hearers today, we have the privilege and thrill of knowing we can have access to that Spirit right now. Because Jesus is who He said He was and did what He said He'd do, we can be fulfilled. Our shame can be undone. Our thirst can be satisfied. "If anyone is thirsty, let [her] come to me and drink" (v. 37).

What does it mean to have streams of living water flowing in you? What feelings came to your mind as you read that?

It makes me feel hopeful, full, light, comforted. I don't have to go back to the "well" of myself, of the things I use to try to fill the void or cover my shame again and again and again and again. Instead, I have the answer. I don't have to cover my shame—the Holy Spirit who fills me covers it for me.

Close out today, praying and thanking God for His Spirit—the living water He gives us that is like a stream flowing from deep within us.

WHERE TO GO WHEN IT WON'T GO AWAY
REVELATION 21:1-6

Every time I think I've just shared my favorite passage of Scripture with you, I get to the next one and I'm like, "OH, YEAH, NO! THIS IS THE BEST!"

Revelation 21 is a place I've gone to camp out so many times in my life—mainly in those seasons when still-here suffering and still-fresh grief and still-surprising pain interrupt my life. Those times when I know I have a stream of living water flowing from deep within me, but I don't feel like I do because though Jesus has been glorified, He hasn't finished glorifying me yet. Though Jesus has removed the stains of my shame, I still think about them sometimes.

Revelation 21 is this too-good-to-be-true-but-the-truest-thing-there-is reminder that when this life is over, our shame won't just be undone but destroyed. Our sadness won't have the ability to resurface when we're weak because we won't be weak. We'll be fully new, fully satisfied, fully whole.

READ REVELATION 21:1-6. Here we're reading John's vision of the new creation. What did John see in verse 1?

Like many of you, as a child I felt concerned that heaven would be everyone standing in rows, perhaps in coordinated robes, singing "I Could Sing of Your Love Forever"—forever. I mean I liked the song, but I was hoping for a little more from my everlasting life. So I can't tell you the level of comfort that washed over me when I learned we wouldn't spend eternity as ghostly, bored spirits singing hymns. No. The Bible, right here, plain as day, tells us that there will be a new heaven and a new earth.

Many of the things we love about earth, the created things we enjoy today, will be back but better than ever. All things will be new and improved because the sting of death and the consequences of sin will no longer taint them. Think about that!

What do these verses tell us about God's dwelling?

I'm about to go home for a visit and am so excited to be with my family. I want to be full-body hugging my little sister in fuzzy socks by a fireplace. I want to hear my mom's laugh and watch my dad fight with their maltipoo over whatever she's got in her mouth. I want the with-ness. I want to be under their roof. What is better than dwelling with the people you love?

We get to have that with God but perfected. No conflict. No hurt feelings. No tiptoeing around differing worldviews or triggering topics. We will dwell with our Father, and He will dwell with us. Perfect family for all of forever.

LOOK BACK AT VERSE 4, and write it out in the space below, soaking in every word.

I don't care how old you are, we all want someone bigger and stronger and better than us to wipe our tears and end our pain.

Go back up to what you just hand wrote and scribble out every word of what God tells us will pass away.

Death—gone; grief—goodbye; crying and pain because of things you've done or things you've had done to you, or things you've thought or things people have thought about you—passed away. Gone forever.

What a hope. What a joy. And it's true.

LOOK AT REVELATION 21:5, and then flip back to 2 Corinthians 5:17. What do these verses both tell us?

Those of us in Christ are new. We already are. We're not waiting till "then." We can already live free from shame when we remember and believe how powerful God's forgiveness is. Whatever your shame is, whatever your sin is—it is forgiven through the already-happened-death of Jesus just as completely as it will be forgiven forever. The difference is that some day, not only will we be new but everything will be new. Everything. Our physical brains will be new. Our trauma-responses and memories and PTSD we carry with us—they will be gone.

For the Christian right now, shame doesn't need to define you. In glory, your shame will have no opportunity to define you. Jesus will make EVERYTHING new.

What does the end of verse 6 tell us about the water of life (living water)?

What do these verses tell you about who God is, what He's like?

Our God is generous. Our God is holy. Our God has all the life and all the power and all the forgiveness and all the water. And He will give it freely to those of us who are His kids. In His home. Forever.

> *Close out this day at the well. Ask the Holy Spirit, deep within you, to help you get through this pre-Revelation 21 day with a mind that is shame-free, joy-filled, and set on the love of Jesus.*

SESSION 3 / GROUP TIME

WATCH

Write down any thoughts, verses, or things you want to remember as you watch the video for Session Three.

_____

_____

_____

_____

_____

_____

_____

_____

_____

_____

_____

_____

_____

_____

_____

_____

_____

_____

_____

_____

To access the video teaching sessions, use the instructions in the back of your Bible study book.

DISCUSS

The Samaritan woman may have carried shame because of her ethnicity and culture. Have you ever experienced anything like that?

This session's main idea is "Jesus gives living water to thirsty hearts." What did you learn in this session about living water and being satisfied?

What are some things you thirst for that will never satisfy?

In what ways do you identify with the woman at the well? How is your story similar to hers?

How can you help someone in your life see his or her need for living water this week?

JESUS SAID, "EVERYONE WHO DRINKS FROM THIS WATER WILL GET THIRSTY AGAIN. BUT WHOEVER DRINKS FROM THE WATER THAT I WILL GIVE HIM WILL NEVER GET THIRSTY AGAIN. IN FACT, THE WATER I WILL GIVE HIM WILL BECOME A WELL OF WATER SPRINGING UP IN HIM FOR ETERNAL LIFE."

JOHN 4:13-14

PRAY

Thank God for making a way for us to be healed and whole and for giving us the most beautiful and hopeful Revelation 21 future. Pray specifically that God would provide opportunities for you to share the living water with others. Ask His Spirit to show you what that might look like individually and as a group.

4

ASHAMED PETER

JESUS GIVES SECOND CHANCES

"FOLLOW ME,"
HE TOLD THEM,
"AND I WILL
MAKE YOU FISH
FOR PEOPLE."
IMMEDIATELY
THEY LEFT
THEIR NETS AND
FOLLOWED HIM.

MATTHEW 4:19-20

MEMORY VERSE

BEWARE THE SHAME REEL

MATTHEW 4:18-22; 14:22-33; LUKE 5:1-11; GALATIANS 2:11-14

I don't know who came up with the term "shame reel," but it's something I refer to every once in a while. Like, "Oh, let's not talk about anything that happened in 2020 or 2021. Everything from those years is in the shame reel."

I don't know about you, but I do my best to ignore, avoid, and erase all memories and evidence of those memories from my shame reel. Sometimes shame-reel memories are small things like that hairstyle that makes you cringe every time you see a photo of yourself or the way you dressed when you didn't have to leave the house (and forgot to dress differently when you were allowed back out into the world).

But then there were the more intense struggles during those days, many of them internal, including loneliness and isolation, mental health issues, and strain on relationships along with stress created by vastly different opinions— and so many other things.

Do you have anything like that in your reel? I think everyone has core memories that make them grimace. Everyone has a shame reel.

In the space provided, describe one of the most uncomfortable moments from your shame reel. Feel free to use pig Latin, invisible ink, or just write it really tiny and then immediately scribble it out, so no one will see what you've written.

As the not-proud owner of a very robust shame reel, I can't tell you how much comfort I find in the life of Peter.

Peter—fisherman, disciple Peter. Are you familiar with him? Refresher: He's the guy Jesus walked with and loved who was used by God to start the Christian church as we know it, *after* so much shame-reel worthy behavior, and *after* he literally denied even knowing Jesus. That guy. But I'm getting ahead of myself.

Let's start in Matthew.

OPEN YOUR BIBLE, AND READ MATTHEW 4:18-22. What was Peter* doing when Jesus invited him to follow?

How long did it take Peter to decide to follow Jesus?

Reflect on your own calling. If you're a follower of Jesus, how long did it take you to decide you were going to commit your life to Christ once you became aware of the truth of the gospel? What did that look like for you? If you're not a follower of Jesus, what drew you to pick up this Bible study? What is it about the story of Jesus calling people to Himself that attracts you?

> *Note: Peter is also called Simon in the Bible. Simon is his actual name; Peter is a sort of nickname Jesus gave him later on. Sometimes you'll see him referred to as Simon, or as Simon Peter, or as Peter. Kind of like how sometimes my husband calls me Scarlet, but other times, at my request, he calls me "Savant Scrawls Prolific Author." That's how my name is saved in his phone, actually. I did it. I saved my name that way. Moving on.

READ LUKE 5:1-11. Many believe this is the same incident, described in two different Gospels.

> How did Peter react in Luke's version of the story when Jesus miraculously filled his fishing nets with fish?

> How did you respond when you first recognized God's power and holiness?

> In Session Two, we looked at a similar response to God's holiness in Isaiah 6. What do Isaiah's and Peter's responses have in common?

I love the similarity. I love how two totally different people—one a prophet, the other a fisherman—both fell before a perfect God and cried out about their sinfulness and unworthiness.

I've often been called out for being self-deprecating, or making fun of myself. It's something I learned early on. It puts people at ease, for sure. Mostly, it puts me at ease!

It's also fun to make fun of yourself because you can be funny but at no one's expense but your own. You'll probably agree only having known me for a few sessions on paper and in video that it's my go-to.

But self-deprecation is not humility. Not even close. It's not godliness. It's a joke. It's a way to cope. It's actually kind of a mask.

> When have you put on the mask of self-deprecation? Why do you think we're tempted to live this way?

True humility might sound similar, but it's beautifully different. Humility's motive isn't protection or relief or a laugh. Humility is free of motives altogether. It's just a sweet, surrendered recognition of our true condition and God's true greatness.

> What similarities do you notice in how Jesus responded to Peter's humility with how God responded to Isaiah's?

In Isaiah, we see an explicit assurance of forgiveness. In Peter's story, we see an invitation to follow.

Bible scholar Thabiti Anyabwile makes such a powerful observation. He writes, "Uniquely, here is a holiness that comes to sinners. Rather than going away, Jesus says, 'Join me.' Here is a holiness that uses a confessing sinner in its mission. Here is holiness that not only calls the sinner but *commissions the sinner* to become a fisher of men. Here is holiness so stunningly beautiful it causes a man to leave everything for its sake. It gives the former sinner a new purpose, direction, and call."[1]

Jesus called Peter to fish for people (v. 10). Fishing for people is a metaphor for evangelism. So cool. Jesus's metaphor was one Peter understood well as a fisherman. While the call to make disciples is for all of us who follow Jesus, Peter's call was delivered in a format specific to his current place in life.

> How have you felt God calling you to use your specific skills and place in life to make disciples? How have you seen others your age do that?

> Are you pursuing what God has set before you or nudged you toward? If so, how? If not, what step can you take in that direction this week?

As you read this next part, keep in mind that this was later in Peter's time as a disciple of Jesus. If you flip back beginning in Matthew 4, when Peter began following Jesus, you see all the rapid-fire miracles and huge events he was part of as he walked with Jesus. He saw miraculous healings (Matt. 4:23-25), the Sermon on the Mount (Matt. 5–7), Jesus calming a storm (Matt. 8:23-27), John the Baptist's beheading (Matt. 14:1-12), and the feeding of the five thousand (Matt. 14:13-21). That's a lot.

READ MATTHEW 14:22-33. List all the emotions you imagine the disciples, and specifically Peter, experienced while this was happening.

What are a few reasons Peter might have experienced shame in this passage?

Shame isn't just a feeling you have internally when one of your many screen-distractions runs out of battery. Shame can be public. And doesn't that make it exponentially more awful? When Peter's focus was on Jesus's power, he got to experience a miracle. But as soon as he took his eyes off Jesus and put them back on the storm, he started sinking. And all the disciples witnessed him sink.

READ GALATIANS 2:11-14 (keeping in mind that Cephas was yet another name for Peter). In this passage, what was Paul calling Peter out for?

Peter was being hypocritical in this passage. The *CSB Study Bible* calls it "fear-based hypocrisy."[2] Despite the fact that Peter had received a vision from God instructing him to fellowship with Gentiles, he allowed the opinions of others to sway his behavior, which in turn swayed the believers around him.

Do you ever find yourself behaving differently or hiding things or (cough cough, hi!) being self-deprecating because you are so concerned with what other people think of you?

We can learn so much from Peter's life as we seek to live lives free of shame, can't we? When we look at the people around us or the storms we're in or the fish we need to catch, we'll sink, we'll be embarrassed, or we'll behave in ways we're ashamed of. But what happens when we look at our Savior? For Peter, it was literally looking at Jesus's face. For us today, it's not quite that literal.

How can we look to Jesus when we feel shame?

And what happens when we do? We experience peace, salvation, and miracles.

Close out this day by asking Jesus—the Remover of our shame, the Holy One who comes to sinners—to help you fix your eyes on Him today, not on your shame reel or future fears or current to-dos.

KITTEN POSTERS ON DETERMINATION

MATTHEW 16:13-18

I went to school in the nineties and early two thousands when motivational posters were a real and prevalent part of everyday life. Nowadays, with all the nineties throwback, I see Gen Z poking their fun (I'm for you Gen Z and am a quiet appreciator of your TikTok humor), making insulting or boring quotes into "motivational" phone backgrounds. But when the glossy paper posters lined the walls of my Christian high school, there was nothing ironic about them.

I remember a giant poster of a kitten hanging off the side of a cliff with the word "DETERMINATION," or something like that, in all caps. Most of the posters were forgettable or painfully cheesy, but there was one that I thought about when class felt boring. One that crossed my mind at night when I was trapped in my existential, angsty swirl.

It was hanging over the big white board in my history teacher's class, and all it said was what I now know is a quote attributed to Einstein: "What is right is not always popular; what is popular is not always right." And I remember that teacher explaining that if everyone is happy with you, you are probably not actually living for Jesus.

I stressed about whether or not it was OK that I was mildly popular (after having been severely unpopular). I wondered if Jesus could possibly be pleased with me/accept me/love me even though I wasn't actively being persecuted as one of His followers.

Think about the people in your life who don't follow Jesus. Who do you think they would say Jesus is?

How would you answer the question, "Who do you say that I am?" if Jesus were to ask you right now?

NOW, READ MATTHEW 16:13-16. When Jesus asked Peter what people said about who He was, how did Peter respond?

My first few years of being a Christian, I wrestled so much with assurance of my salvation. I wanted a formula that would guarantee my saved status, but I lived lite so consumed by what people thought of me—the teacher with the motivational posters, my friends, my parents—that I often found my good works were self-centered. I wondered if I really, truly could claim Jesus as the Messiah or if I really, truly only wanted to do what it seemed "good girls" did.

Can you relate? When have you caught yourself acting a certain way because of others' opinions rather than God's?

READ MATTHEW 16:17. Who did Jesus tell Peter was responsible for him recognizing that Jesus was the Messiah?

Isn't that so comforting? Peter didn't believe because he was a super-awesome five-star person all the fishermen admired. He believed, not because flesh and blood revealed it to him, but God in heaven.

In the space below, rewrite verse 17, and meditate on the beauty that God is the Revealer and the Savior and the Keeper of your soul.

READ MATTHEW 16:18-19. List of all the things Jesus said He would do through and for Peter.

Look up the verses in the chart and note what Jesus promises He will do in and through and for His followers.

PASSAGE	WHAT JESUS WILL DO FOR YOU
Isaiah 40:31	
Matthew 16:24-25	
John 14:27	
John 15:9-15	
John 16:13-14	
Romans 5:10	
1 John 1:9	

Jesus offers us life, joy, peace, forgiveness, reconciliation—all the good stuff we long for.

We don't have to live in fear of what other people think or be ashamed of the times we've taken our eyes off of Jesus. Instead, we remember what He has revealed to us. He's given us eyes to see who He is. He's given us promises of what He will do. God reveals Himself to us, calls us, saves us, and does the work of transforming us into His likeness, bit by bit.

> *Close out this day thanking God for carrying the weight of your sin and the shame of your past, and praise Him for the beautiful future He has in store for all of us sinners who believe.*

PETER DENIES JESUS
MATTHEW 26:31-35, 69-75; JOHN 18:15-18; ROMANS 5:6-8

The only thing I've ever been good at predicting has been how long pets would thrive in our home. I have three little girls, and we've tested out a variety of animals. The most recent death I predicted was that of a caterpillar my youngest found on the patio. He had a name, a specified jar, and a collection of leaves. But he was a goner. I knew it immediately.

I gave him three days max. He made it two.

Caterpillar life spans might be my only area of expertise when it comes to conjecture. In today's passage though, we'll look at a prediction Jesus made about Peter and how that played out. Hint: Jesus is always right.

READ MATTHEW 26:31-35. What prediction did Jesus make in these verses?

What was Peter's reaction to Jesus's prediction?

If you were Peter in this moment, what emotions would you feel?

You know, I never think much about the fact that Jesus didn't just love and use and save Peter after his three-time denial—He called it! He knew Peter would deny Him. The whole time Peter followed Jesus, He spoke salvation and promise and hope and purpose over Peter, *before* Peter failed Him. He did so *knowing* Peter would fail Him. Does that comfort your wound-up-tight, overthinking mind like it does mine?

What are you carrying shame about right now? Explain.

Hear me out here: Consider the reality that Jesus knew you'd fail the way you did before it even happened. And He called you to Himself anyway. He is still calling you to Himself anyway, right now as you read this. In this way, we have an advantage over Peter. We know the end of the story. We know Jesus died and rose again to declare us forgiven and clean and His.

READ ROMANS 5:6-8. When did Jesus die for us? (Hint: while we were still _____.)

How can we be ashamed when we remember that He loved before we loved? How can we focus on our failures when Jesus declared us forgiven and clean and His *while we were still sinners*?

READ MATTHEW 26:69-75. When Peter was accused of being one of Jesus's followers, how did he respond?

When have you lied to distance yourself from a person or situation that embarrassed you or made you feel threatened? Explain.

What do you think Jesus wants to say to your heart about that situation?

John's account of this same moment gives us a little more context.

READ JOHN 18:15-18. Note Peter's surroundings at this moment. Where was he? What details did John give about what Peter may have been smelling, feeling, hearing?

It was Peter who cut off the soldier's ear when Jesus was being arrested (v. 10), and just a few verses later, he's denying Jesus completely.

Bring the burdens of your past failures to the Lord. Thank Him for His forgiveness, and rewrite Psalm 103:12 in the space provided.

Looking at the denials of Peter reminds me of so many times when my fear of people overpowered my belief in the all-powerful Jesus. In his book, *When People are Big and God is Small*, Edward T. Welch writes,

> We fear people because they can
> 1. expose and humiliate us,
> 2. ridicule and reject us, and
> 3. attack, threaten, or oppress us.
>
> These three reasons have one thing in common: they see people as "bigger" (that is, more powerful and significant) than God, and, out of the fear that creates in us, we give other people the power to tell us what to feel, think, and do.[3]

As you close out this day, write a prayer below, asking God to help you see how much bigger and more powerful He is than the people He created. Ask Him to help you live in light of that and ask for His help in fighting the shame you feel over how you acted when you made people big and God small.

SHAME-REVERSING POWER

JOHN 21:1-19

The passage you are about to read is so beautiful. It has shame-reversing power. Open up to John 21. In this chapter, Jesus had already been crucified and buried. He'd already risen from the dead, securing life for those who believe, and He had started visiting with people before ascending into heaven.

John 21 isn't just a random conversation Jesus had during His ministry. This conversation between Jesus and Peter that we're about to look at happened after Christ's ministry on earth, after He was mocked and tortured and killed for the salvation of humanity, and after Peter had denied Him, swearing and cursing that he didn't know the man (Matt. 26:74).

So, get your mind there. Imagine that you are Peter, and you're having an actual in-person conversation over breakfast with your back-from-the-dead Teacher/Friend/Savior, whom you denied, and denied, and denied again.

READ JOHN 21:1-14. How is this similar to the story we read in Luke 5 of Peter's calling to follow Jesus?

Using the five senses, describe some of what Peter might have been experiencing physically at this moment.

• Smell:

• Touch/Feel:

• Taste:

• See:

• Hear:

What moments from his past do you think those sensations brought to mind? Do you think those were pleasant memories for him? Explain.

When we carry shame in our hearts, we may avoid good things to avoid remembering the times when we failed, right? Peter, dripping wet from his swim in the sea, walked up to a charcoal fire Jesus had prepared for His disciples' breakfast.

Science tells us that smell, memory, and emotion are closely tied together due to the anatomy of our brains.[4] John specifically mentioned a charcoal fire in John 18 and 21. These two instances are the only two times in the whole Bible where that phrase is used. Charcoal fires have a specific scent. Love it or hate it, you can probably remember a time when you've been around a charcoal fire. Maybe a summer barbecue comes to mind for you.

The Bible does not explicitly say this, and I want to be clear on that, but I believe our Creator is intimately knowledgeable about how our brains work. He created brains, after all! He knows the memories we associate with each smell. How beautiful and gracious that He would give Peter the opportunity to reset those memory connections in his mind!

READ JOHN 21:15-19. What question did Jesus ask Peter?

How many times did He ask it?

You know when you get into an argument with a sibling or friend or even your parents? Arguments, misunderstandings, or conflict, if serious enough, can fracture relationships beyond repair. You don't have to travel too far from the preschool playground to learn that. Conflict can destroy affection. So, what a blow it must have been to Peter for Jesus to ask, "Do you love me?" Peter stood by the fire, hearing this question, knowing how he'd failed Jesus just before His death, and likely remembering that Jesus had predicted that's what he would do.

I can look back on my life and remember multiple situations where I wronged someone and then was faced with the reality that they'd witnessed it or heard about it. I'd been made.

In the top two instances that come to my mind, I didn't receive forgiveness from the people involved. My actions ended our friendship—a just consequence for my failures. But here we see Peter and Jesus together. They were eating breakfast. Peter knew he was unworthy. Undeserved restoration.

REREAD VERSE 17. When Jesus symbolically asked Peter, "Do you love me," for the third time, how does the Bible say Peter felt?

Every time I have been confronted with how my mistakes have hurt someone else, I have felt that gut-wrenching sort of grief. It's like dropping something precious and watching it shatter into a million pieces, beyond repair.

How did Jesus respond three times to Peter's declaration?

Despite the grief and shame Peter undoubtedly carried, Jesus gave Him a role, a purpose, and a second chance.

Describe how Jesus has given you each of the following:

• A role:

• A purpose:

• A second chance:

In some translations, it's "feed my sheep." In others, it's "lambs." The translation from the Greek is a little complex, but all of it points to shepherding, tending to, and the like.

Now, in the same way Jesus wasn't telling Peter to cast a physical net in the ocean to "fish for people," Jesus wasn't talking about literal sheep needing breakfast.

So, what does sheep feeding look like in your life? Who are you discipling or serving? If nothing comes to mind immediately, ask God to show you what it would look like for you to feed sheep.

Look at the last two words in verse 19. What did Jesus tell Peter to do?

If you flip back to Day One to that first passage we studied (Matt. 4:18-22), you can see how beautifully full circle this "Do you love me . . . feed my sheep" moment was for Peter.

What did Jesus say to Peter and his brother, Andrew, in Matthew 4:19, when they first met?

Isn't that amazing? Jesus said the same exact thing on both occasions: "Follow me." Jesus called Peter to follow Him and fish for people and feed sheep. Even when Peter messed it all up, he was not disqualified from serving Jesus. Even when his actions could have destroyed the relationship, Jesus kept Peter in His purpose and His love.

Can you think of an area of your life where your failures or mistakes have caused you to feel disqualified? Close out this day by writing out a prayer of renewed commitment to feed the sheep God has called you to feed and follow Him where He leads you. Thank Him for second and third and millionth chances, and move forward with gospel-given joy.

HOW GOSPEL-POWERED HUMILITY ERASES SHAME

1 PETER 5:6-11

Casting all your cares on him, because he cares about you.

1 PETER 5:7

I used to be so frustrated by this verse. I wanted to experience it. I wanted to obey it. I just didn't understand it. Many times I tried casting, but I couldn't stop caring. I'd throw up my figurative arms, full of figurative cares, and wonder why the peace thing wasn't kicking in.

But as I've learned to release my shame, I've also learned to embrace God's Word. I've learned that studying Scripture slowly and routinely and fully is not a box to check, but it's the very key to transformation—the very way to make peace with my past.

It wasn't until I looked one verse before verse 7 that I understood how to cast my cares on the Lord and why I even could.

> **READ 1 PETER 5:6-7.** Copy the first two words you see in the space below. (If the version you're using puts a "Therefore" or a "So" at the beginning, skip that word and write the next two).

Shame and humility are antonyms that we often treat like synonyms. As we discussed on Day One of this session, being humble isn't wallowing in humiliation; it's having an awareness of your true status in light of God's goodness. Isn't it so beautiful, then, that Peter is the one who wrote these verses, under the inspiration of the Holy Spirit? Peter, aware of Jesus's divinity, aware of how he'd failed his friend, and aware that he'd been forgiven and given a second chance said, "Humble yourselves, therefore, under the mighty hand of God, so that he may exalt you at the proper time" (v. 6).

We can all personalize that.

In the space below, humble yourself. Write down a few memories of times you've seen the mighty hand of God at work in your life.

If you look again at verse 7 in light of verse 6, it is so much easier to cast your cares. Casting is really about remembering who is in control. We can humble ourselves, surrendering the cares we can't carry ourselves, when we remember and believe the gospel. I love how Tim Keller explains the life-changing power of the gospel. It came across my Facebook® feed again just this morning.

The Christian Gospel is that I am so flawed that Jesus had to die for me, yet I am so loved and valued that Jesus was glad to die for me. This leads to deep humility and deep confidence at the same time. It undermines both swaggering and sniveling.[5]

If you picked up this Bible study, you might feel that you're more prone to the "sniveling." You might feel far from swagger and overwhelmed with shame. Or maybe you got pressured into coming to this study, and you actually feel like you're doing pretty awesome. The incredible thing is that the "deep humility" Keller referenced here gets us away from both of those two unhealthy extremes and gives us a confidence that comes from the gratitude of being given the world-changing grace of Jesus.

READ 1 PETER 5:8-11. In concluding his letter, what warning does Peter give in verses 8 and 9?

Having studied Peter's relationship with Jesus, why is this significant?

You probably wouldn't take violin lessons from someone who has never played or ask a math tutor to help you with English. It's a lot easier for us to take someone's advice when she's got experience. Honestly, I studied 1 Peter all my life in Christian schools and college, but I never considered who wrote the letter. I never considered that the one urging me to resist the devil and stand firm in my faith was someone who hadn't always resisted or stood firm. When he wrote about prowling lions and suffering and resisting, he knew what he was talking about.

What hope does Peter offer in verses 10-11?

How stunning. How powerful. The guy who denied Jesus, who cowered in fear rather than standing firm, gives us a warning, followed by incredible comfort. God will "restore, establish, strengthen, and support [us] after [we] have suffered a little while" (v. 10).

Using what you learned this week, how did we see Peter experience restoration, establishment, strengthening, and support?

Have you experienced these comforts after struggling with shame? In the space below, try to recall and record times you have experienced these gifts from the Lord.

- Restoration:

- Establishment:

- Strengthening:

- Support:

Close out this day, thanking God for these good gifts we have because of the mercy of Jesus.

SESSION 4 / GROUP TIME

WATCH

Write down any thoughts, verses, or things you want to remember as you watch the video for Session Four.

_____

_____

_____

_____

_____

_____

_____

_____

_____

_____

_____

_____

_____

_____

_____

_____

_____

_____

_____

_____

_____

_____

To access the video teaching sessions, use the instructions in the back of your Bible study book.

DISCUSS

On Day One, we read about when Jesus met Peter and said, "Follow me." Take some time to share about what your life looked like when you were introduced to Jesus.

This session's main idea is "Jesus gives second chances." If you're comfortable, share a story of a time God gave you a second chance.

"FOLLOW ME," HE TOLD THEM, "AND I WILL MAKE YOU FISH FOR PEOPLE." IMMEDIATELY THEY LEFT THEIR NETS AND FOLLOWED HIM.

MATTHEW 4:19-20

Flip back to the chart you filled out on Day Two (p. 70), showing what Jesus promises to do in and through His followers. Which of these promises resonates most with you? Why?

In what ways do you personally identify with Peter? What, in your history with the Lord, brings a feeling of shame to your mind? What have you learned that Jesus wants to do with your shame by studying Peter this week?

Jesus used Peter to build the church as we know it. If you're involved in your local church, how has God wired you to serve? If you're not yet involved, what do you sense God is leading you to do within your church?

PRAY

Thank God for allowing His children to do kingdom work and live with purpose, even though we don't deserve that joy and privilege. Pray specifically that you, as a group, would walk in joyful obedience as you continue to study God's Word together. Ask that the Lord unite your group and remove all shame that is keeping you from service to Him and joy in His calling on your life.

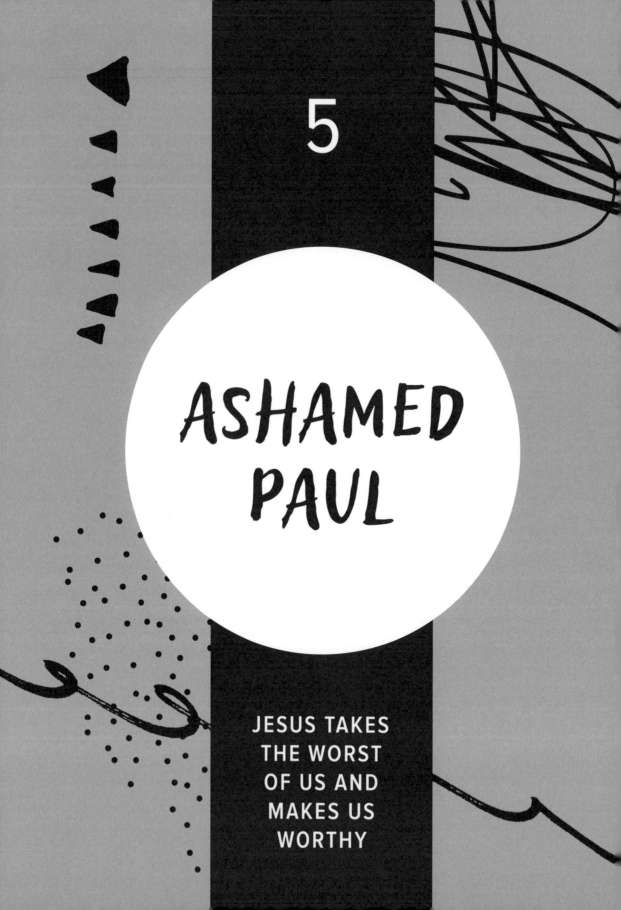

5

ASHAMED PAUL

JESUS TAKES
THE WORST
OF US AND
MAKES US
WORTHY

THIS SAYING IS TRUSTWORTHY
AND DESERVING OF FULL
ACCEPTANCE. "CHRIST JESUS
CAME INTO THE WORLD TO
SAVE SINNERS" — AND I AM
THE WORST OF THEM. BUT I
RECEIVED MERCY FOR THIS
REASON, SO THAT IN ME,
THE WORST OF THEM, CHRIST
JESUS MIGHT DEMONSTRATE
HIS EXTRAORDINARY
PATIENCE AS AN EXAMPLE TO
THOSE WHO WOULD BELIEVE
IN HIM FOR ETERNAL LIFE.

1 TIMOTHY 1:15-16

MEMORY VERSE

SHIPWRECK TATTOOS ON SHIPWRECKED PEOPLE

ACTS 9:1-19

I'm on a plane right now, leaving Atlanta. I was there to speak at a church event north of town and can't stop thinking about a testimony I heard.

One of my favorite things about traveling to speak and share my testimony is getting to talk to women before and after, getting to hear their stories of how Jesus has changed their lives.

Before I went up to speak at this church last night, a woman from the congregation got up to share her story. She had cool, chunky glasses, a spunky haircut, and a full sleeve of tattoos. And she said, "These tattoos are my testimony."

The tattoos depicted a shipwreck. A shipwreck that represented the circumstances and outcome of a life that had let her down. But Jesus redeemed her. He healed her wounds and restored what was broken. She said that when she worships at church and raises her arms, she can see the shipwreck tattoo turned upside down, and it reminds her how Jesus changed everything.

Her story was different from mine. The pain she'd experienced. The losses she'd grieved. But I couldn't help but feel like she was telling my story too. Jesus meets us in our brokenness—however our personal brokenness takes shape.

This week we are looking at one of Scripture's biggest shipwrecked-people-turned-apostle—Paul, also known as Saul.

You've experienced shame in your past? For sure. You've done things or said things you hate remembering? You've *not* done things or *not* said things you keep recalling and regretting? The apostle Paul says to you, "Hold my grape juice." Paul was the worst, and Paul was made new. We can be encouraged by a persecutor turned martyr who got into some actual shipwrecks too.

READ ACTS 9:1-18. What does verse 1 say Paul (remember, Paul is Saul) was doing when he was traveling on this Damascus road?

Pretty intense guy, this Saul/Paul was. Have you ever had so much anger in your heart that you were "breathing threats and murder" against people? Actually, never mind—don't answer that.

When I first learned about Paul, I viewed him as a villain with a big life-changing story. But I didn't think about how Paul must have viewed himself. From his perspective, his murderous threat-breathing was righteous! See, Paul was a Jew. He was part of the elite "God's chosen people" group, the Israelites. He was religious. In fact, he was so religious that he viewed himself as this holy warrior guy who would take down anyone who didn't worship his God his way.

When have you been so convinced you were right or so passionate about something that you would have "taken down" (at least with your words) people who didn't feel the same? Explain.

When Paul heard about this group of people who followed Jesus—people who Paul and others like him thought were crazy, blasphemous, extremists— he justified violence as a way to remedy what he saw.

But his encounter with Jesus changed everything.

When Paul asked who the voice was, what answer did he receive?

I appreciate the clarity here since I'm reading this centuries later as someone who has not hunted down Jesus followers to put them into prison. But imagine how that answer felt to Paul. Not only was it (rightly) accusatory, but Jesus also equated Himself with His followers. He was essentially telling Paul: *You aren't just hurting people who believe in Me. You are persecuting Me. Jesus.*

LOOK AGAIN AT VERSES 10-18. What was the name of the guy God commanded to go help Paul?

How did he respond when the Lord said his name in verse 10, and who does that remind you of from Session Two?

"Here I am, Lord!" "Here I am; send me!" Remember, Isaiah? Isn't it cool and beautiful that when regular people encounter God, their response is service rather than shame?

Ananias was willing to go serve a known murderer, a known persecutor, because God called him by name and told him to.

In verses 15-16, what did God tell Ananias about what would happen to Paul?

Why do you think God told Ananias these things about Paul's future?

Look at verse 18. What happened immediately before Paul got baptized?

God opened Paul's eyes to His holiness, just like He did to Ananias, just like Isaiah, just like me. And Paul walked forward in joyful obedience rather than wallowing in the failures of his past. Incredible.

What do you tend to do or turn to when you are confronted with your sin?

If you have an unhealthy pattern of getting stuck in the sadness of your failures, how might you learn from Paul's example?

Close out this day asking the Holy Spirit to show you how to behave differently in light of the reality that your sins are forgiven.

THE ONLY FIX FOR BROKEN PEOPLE
ACTS 9:20-31; LUKE 18:27

I've dealt with a painful estrangement in my family on and off since I was eighteen years old. The hot and cold of it, the misunderstandings, the severing words, the crying and the praying, and counseling and book dog-earring.

It has been one of the most heartbreaking and deflating things I've ever experienced. I hung around and tried again and again to fix something that wasn't getting fixed. I cycled through hurt and anger and frustration and exasperation and *shame*. So much shame. Aren't I a child of God? Shouldn't my supernatural love be able to fix what's broken? What's wrong with me? What's wrong with my faith?

The cynic in me (that can still pop up when I'm not careful) used to nod in world-weary agreement at the expression, "People never change." *Addicts will always be addicts. Cheaters will always cheat. Never trust a liar.*

And honestly, history and a little life experience often proves those things to be true. But God.

READ ACTS 9:20-25. What did Paul immediately start doing after his conversion?

Why were his listeners astounded?

I can't think of much else that is more powerful proof of a heart-changing God than encountering a heart-changed person. Sure, this side of heaven we'll always be weighed down by sin: redeemed addicts may still struggle against the source of their addiction, repentant cheaters may still feel a draw to cheat, and rescued liars could still feel tempted to lie. But the power of the gospel tells us we're no longer enslaved to those sins because Jesus transforms us out of our slavery to sin. As Paul reminds us in 2 Corinthians 3:17, "Where the Spirit of the Lord is, there is freedom."

> If you are a believer, do you remember how you used to live and function before you became a child of God? What were you like? What has changed?

READ ACTS 9:26-30. How did Jesus's disciples respond to Paul when he tried to join them?

> Have you ever been wary of trusting someone who claimed to be changed? Why or why not?

All of us carry the pains of loving people who are making choices that hurt them and their relationships. A lot of those situations look hopeless and some of them even end in what appears to be hopelessness. The aftermath of some of my stories makes it difficult for me to believe people can change. Though I carry stories of pain and loss, I've also witnessed the miracle of people headed down that path who were redeemed and restored.

> What evidence did Barnabas give to explain Paul's transformation?

> Have you ever seen a dramatic change, similar to Paul's, in someone's life? Maybe it was your life. What evidence would you give that that person had changed? What evidence would someone else give about your life?

Not only did Barnabas cite Paul's preaching "in the name of Jesus," he also said Paul "had seen the Lord" (v. 27). Paul literally saw Jesus. He saw his sin in the light of the One who died to save him from those sins. And he left that encounter a changed man.

NOW, READ VERSE 31. What happened to the churches in the area as Paul and the others who were changed by Jesus shared the good news?

Not only did the church grow in numbers but in strength and in peace. I love verse 31 so much. Praying for the lost, hoping for restoration and healing and unity—it's not pointless.

READ LUKE 18:27, and write it out below. Pay attention to each word and ask the Holy Spirit to help your heart believe it.

The health of the church and the healing of broken people and relationships is not up to us. It is Jesus Christ who changes lives. He uses formerly hopeless people like me and Saul the Persecutor to do it. So, be encouraged. Let go of your shame. Hope in the power of the gospel. Jesus is using you, and the kingdom of heaven can't be defeated.

Close out this day praying for the people you love in those relationships that hurt. Ask in faith for the Lord to strengthen and encourage you, your church, and your community. Ask Him to help you have peace in the things you can't change and trust His power over the rest.

COMPETENT WORSTIES

2 CORINTHIANS 3:4-18; 4:1-6; 5:17

Last year, I published a book called, *You're the Worst Person in the World.* I wrote ten chapters on my worstness in hopes readers might see their own (and maybe laugh with me?). I really wanted #worsties to take off as a hashtag on Instagram, but it hasn't. Apparently, nobody wants to celebrate being the worst. ☺

But one of the things I love about Paul's ministry is the confidence his humility produced. He wasn't trying to hashtag his failures or toot a horn about his wins. His confidence didn't come from himself. That is so powerful because he was very qualified to be an extra-zealous Jew according to the standards of the time (Phil. 3:4-6).

The subheading in today's reading in my Bible is "Paul's Competence." When I see the word *competence*, I feel like I'm about to read a list of special braggy skills on someone's LinkedIn® profile.

> To Whom It May Concern,
>
> My name is Paul, and the following is but a sample of my skills and competencies . . .
>
> - Relentless Work Ethic
> - Collaborative Leadership
> - Written Communication Pro
> - Multilingual (Hebrew, Aramaic, Greek)
>
> - Organizational Know-How
> - Creative, Empathetic Multitasker
> - Extremely Punctual
> - Working Knowledge of Microsoft Excel®

But Paul's second letter to the Corinthian church reads nothing like that.

READ 2 CORINTHIANS 3:4-6. How does Paul say we are made competent? Why do we need to be made competent?

In his letter to the Ephesians, Paul explains that salvation in Jesus is a gift, so no one can boast. But here in 2 Corinthians, he reminds the church members of Corinth then, and us now, that we can't claim that anything comes from us.

NOW, READ VERSES 7-11. Why does Paul say the glory of the law given to Moses is less glorious than the ministry of the Spirit?

If you didn't include it in your answer above, the most breathtaking difference between the law on stone tablets and the ministry of the Spirit is that the law condemned us all.

No one can keep the law perfectly. No one but the glorious, holy God Himself.

Paul goes so far as to tell us we have a front-row seat to God's glory on display through the work of Jesus and the presence of the Holy Spirit with us (2 Cor. 3:12-18).

Doesn't that front-row seat to God's glory on display give us boldness? Doesn't it remind us that Christ has removed the veil so that we can see God's glory more fully, as if a veil has been removed completely (2 Cor. 3:16)? It really does.

Seeing the fullness of God's glory reminds us of our need. It reminds us we can never be worthy on our own. The glory of God, the glory of His covenant, will not fade. Because of this, we can stand boldly because we are "being transformed into the same image from glory to glory" (v. 18) through Jesus.

Speaking of testimony tattoos, I've got a Bible verse reference tattooed on my right wrist:

> *Therefore, if anyone is in Christ, he is a new creation; the old*
> *has passed away, and see, the new has come!*

2 CORINTHIANS 5:17

If you lose sight of that, you may find yourself living under condemnation from a law that you have already been forgiven for breaking. Whether or not you actually feel free of shame, if you have given your life to God and invited Jesus the Savior into your life, you are *already* free! You are *already* new! God's will for you isn't shame, it's glory. He doesn't want to make you hide; He wants to make you like Him.

READ 2 CORINTHIANS 4:1-6. Why do we not give up?

What are we supposed to renounce?

What would it look like if the gospel was unveiled in your life?

See, fighting shame doesn't mean being "shameless" in the negative sense of the word. We who are in Christ know very well how undeserving we are. We know we couldn't live up to God's standard. We know our hearts are deceitful (Jer. 17:9). But we do not have to be ashamed. Jesus has made us clean! He's not overlooking your worstness. He's removed it, canceled it, and exchanged it for His best. We get to wear the blamelessness of Jesus. What a mercy.

> *Close out this day by writing a prayer of gratitude.*
> *Ask the Lord to help your heart's baseline have the joyful,*
> *peaceful rest of one who has truly been redeemed.*

DAY FOUR

FIGHTING SHAME BY LOOKING UP
2 CORINTHIANS 4:7-18; COLOSSIANS 3:2

Grandma Marlene, a rock in my family, died from COVID pneumonia last year. By the time I got the call, I couldn't get there to see her in person, but a nurse called me on FaceTime® and held the phone up so I could say goodbye. But I didn't know what to say. All I remember coming out was "I love you so much, Grandma. Your braids are so pretty. I love you. I love you. I love you. Thank you, Jesus, for my Grandma. Thank you, Jesus . . ."

She died a few minutes later.

My heart is still broken over her death because I miss her presence here. But the way she lived gives me so much confidence in the eternity she always talked about and longed for.

Something she lived by and taught me was Colossians 3:2: "Set your minds on things above, not on earthly things." That was her secret. That was where her near-constant joy came from.

Her life circumstances were up and down, but she lived a life full of gratitude. She raved about trees in her yard and birds in her bird bath. She sang songs to Jesus and walked around with a unique and radiant confidence because her mind was set on eternal things.

When I read today's passage, written by Paul, under the inspiration of the Holy Spirit, I think about the life I watched Grandma Marlene live out to the very end. I want you to have the same radiant confidence and joy that Jesus gave her.

Who in your life lives with radiant confidence and joy in Jesus? How do they inspire you? Consider writing a note or sending a text to tell them!

READ 2 CORINTHIANS 4:7-18. In the chart below, use today's passage to record our state in light of each circumstance. I'll do the first one for you.

THOUGH WE ARE . . .	WE ARE . . .
Afflicted in every way	Not crushed
Perplexed	
Persecuted	
Struck down	

Which of these realities feels most relatable in your life right now? Whichever one it is, copy down what you wrote in the box and how it applies to your situation. (For example, someone might write: "I am afflicted in every way. I'm not getting along with my brother; I failed my English final; I'm fighting with my best friend; but I am not crushed because God is . . . ")

NOW, ZERO IN ON VERSE 10. What does that verse say we carry in our bodies, and what then can be displayed in our bodies?

When I lost Grandma Marlene, I suffered so many other afflictions too. I felt afflicted in every way . . .

But not crushed.

When have you felt crushed over something that happened to you or around you? How do these verses shift your perspective on that situation? Can you see how God came through for you, even when you felt crushed? Explain.

We all carry the curse with us, don't we? We live in a world broken by sin, a world tainted with shame. If you didn't feel it pre-2020, you feel it now. A phrase I used to describe myself during that season of loss and affliction was "world weary." We are world weary, but we are never without hope.

LOOK AT VERSES 14 AND 15. What did Paul say can extend through us?

Where does the thanksgiving at the end of verse 15 come from?

Jesus's resurrection changed everything. The ultimate curse of our sin is death, and when He came back to life, He showed the world His power over it. If God can raise Jesus from the dead, if God can forgive the sins of Paul the persecutor, can't He forgive you? Can't He heal you from how others have sinned against you?

Of course He can! He has world-making power. Jesus-resurrecting power. And He uses that power to love us. Setting our minds on this amazing reality produces what verse fifteen says it will—gratitude. It makes us thankful people. And we can't be thankful and shameful at the same time.

I love looking at 2 Corinthians 4:18 and Colossians 3:2 side by side.

So we do not focus on what is seen, but on what is unseen. For what is seen is temporary, but what is unseen is eternal.

2 CORINTHIANS 4:18

Set your minds on things above, not on earthly things.

COLOSSIANS 3:2

We can set our minds on things above and focus on eternity, on the goodness of the Lord, on the unseen, because while the things that have brought us shame are temporary, the love of our all-powerful God through Jesus lasts forever.

Finish today's time with Jesus by reflecting on 2 Corinthians 4:16-18. Pray a prayer, reminding yourself exactly why it is that we do not give up— exactly why it is that we can shake off shame, hold on to thankfulness, and hope in the power of God.

SHAME TURNED TESTIMONY
I TIMOTHY 1:12-17

Today's passage has a beautiful heading in my CSB Bible: "Paul's Testimony." Man, I love hearing people's testimonies. I love the colorful ones like Paul's and the ones that point to faithful families passing down the good news.

The older I get, the more testimonies of my own I rack up.

I've been a striver in need of rest who made a commitment to Jesus.

I've been a hurting girl who was healed and experienced God's mercy.

I've been panicked and wanted comfort and safety more than I wanted God. But He reminded me of His love for me and my purpose for Him.

I've been world-weary, too tired and too sad and too grieving to pursue the Lord, but He used people and prayer and His Word to pursue me, and hold me, and give me joyful endurance.

God is constantly turning brokenness into beauty. He turns shame into testimonies.

READ I TIMOTHY 1:12-17. What words did Paul use to describe who he was before?

Can you identify with any of those descriptions? If so, write about it below. What did your specific struggles look like before you were changed by Jesus? If you don't know Him yet, what is weighing you down right now?

How did Paul describe what changed him?

Why did Paul say he received mercy?

How does your testimony demonstrate God's "extraordinary patience"?

"'Christ Jesus came into the world to save sinners'—and I am the worst of them" (v. 15). What a stunningly beautiful sentiment when spoken in earnest. But what a difficult thing to admit.

We spend our entire lives justifying bad behavior and trying to convince ourselves that we're worthy. Or we distract ourselves away from thinking about it, but the reality is, it's not working. And it takes a lot of mental gymnastics to try to convince ourselves that we're good people.

After Paul's encounter with Jesus, he had the truth figured out. He was physically blinded, but his eyes were opened to his need, his weakness, his glaring failure of letting self-righteousness consume him.

He was finally able to see the giant Jesus-sized need in his life, and Jesus was there to fill it.

What a wonder that when we are able to be honest with ourselves about our own weaknesses, we are most poised to be free.

Do you have a testimony? A God story? An "I was this,
but now I'm that" to share? Try to put it into words in the
space provided. If you're a visual person, draw a picture here or
on the next page of what your life looked like before Christ
and how following Him changed it. As you draw or write,
ask God how He wants you to use your God story
to tell others about Him.

SESSION 5 / GROUP TIME

WATCH

Write down any thoughts, verses, or things you want to remember as you watch the video for Session Five.

To access the video teaching sessions, use the instructions in the back of your Bible study book.

DISCUSS

This week, we studied Paul and his one-hundred-eighty-degree turn of a testimony. What is the most dramatic one-eighty testimony you've ever heard?

This session's main idea is "Jesus takes the worst of us and makes us worthy." When have you gotten to a point where you had to acknowledge your "worstness"?

Do you have a Grandma Marlene in your life? Someone who, though imperfect, shows you what it looks like to live in light of eternity? Describe that person.

PRAY

Thank God for forgiving sinners like us and allowing us to take part in the beautiful love story He's writing. Thank Him for saving people like Paul. Thank Him for the one-hundred-eighty-degree testimonies and the quieter ones. Thank Him for what He is doing in your story and in your group. Spend the remainder of your time in prayer. Pray specifically that you, as a group, would spend the rest of this week reflecting the unveiled gospel with hearts free of shame.

THIS SAYING IS TRUSTWORTHY AND DESERVING OF FULL ACCEPTANCE: "CHRIST JESUS CAME INTO THE WORLD TO SAVE SINNERS" — AND I AM THE WORST OF THEM. BUT I RECEIVED MERCY FOR THIS REASON, SO THAT IN ME, THE WORST OF THEM, CHRIST JESUS MIGHT DEMONSTRATE HIS EXTRAORDINARY PATIENCE AS AN EXAMPLE TO THOSE WHO WOULD BELIEVE IN HIM FOR ETERNAL LIFE.

1 TIMOTHY 1:15-16

In this session's video, the author covers topics that could be difficult for some teen girls. Please preview the content beforehand and take into consideration the needs of each of the girls in your group before showing the video in its entirety. See page 137 for context notes.

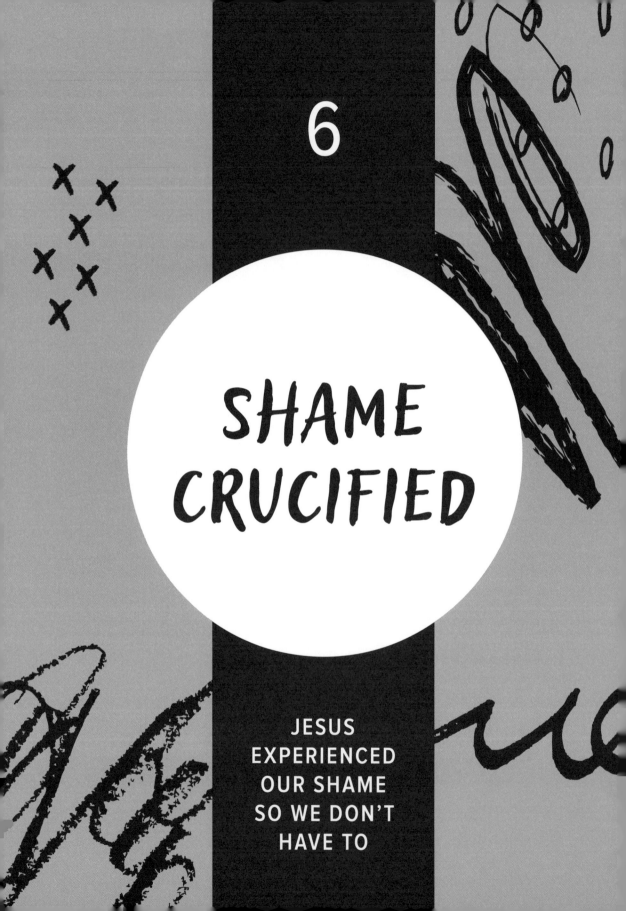

6

SHAME CRUCIFIED

JESUS
EXPERIENCED
OUR SHAME
SO WE DON'T
HAVE TO

THEREFORE, SINCE WE ALSO HAVE SUCH A LARGE CLOUD OF WITNESSES SURROUNDING US, LET US LAY ASIDE EVERY HINDRANCE AND THE SIN THAT SO EASILY ENSNARES US. LET US RUN WITH ENDURANCE THE RACE THAT LIES BEFORE US, KEEPING OUR EYES ON JESUS, THE PIONEER AND PERFECTER OF OUR FAITH. FOR THE JOY THAT LAY BEFORE HIM, HE ENDURED THE CROSS, DESPISING THE SHAME, AND SAT DOWN AT THE RIGHT HAND OF THE THRONE OF GOD.

HEBREWS 12:1-2

WE ARE GUILTY

ROMANS 1:16-32; 3:9-24

After Jesus changed the apostle Paul's life, Paul spent the rest of it traveling around, as the Holy Spirit led, sharing the gospel and building the church. Remember, this is the same guy whose past involved imprisoning Jesus's followers and even having them killed. But God took his zeal and redirected it. He took Paul's sin and forgave it.

Paul had so many failures and sins he could have looked back on, but instead he preached the good news of Jesus with confidence. Paul knew his past, so he wasn't confident in himself. He was confident in his Savior.

READ ROMANS 1:16-17. What was Paul "not ashamed" of?

Have you ever found yourself ashamed of the gospel, or embarrassed to share your faith? Why do you think that is?

NOW, READ ROMANS 1:18-25. What do these verses say about our guilt?

Perhaps that's not the most encouraging passage. But it is crucial and true.

When we're faced with the gospel, we see that we are guilty. We deserve God's wrath. It's true. We are "without excuse," because just like this description in Romans, we have lacked gratitude, walked in darkness, and worshiped things that are not God so many times. And that means, in so many ways, that the shame we feel isn't invalid. Which only makes it more amazing when God makes it go away.

READ ROMANS 1:26-32. What stands out to you? Write down any of the unrighteous things in the list that you currently struggle with.

What messages of shame have you spoken over yourself because of those struggles?

It's a painful list to read. I can say confidently that some of that resonates with me. We are wired to worship, and if we aren't worshiping the One who is worthy, we will worship ourselves. That leads to the pursuit of the things in that long list, which inevitably leads to guilt and shame.

NOW READ ROMANS 3:9-20. According to this passage, is anyone justified by the works of the law?

Have you ever lived like you could be justified by your works? What did that look like in your life?

READ ROMANS 3:21-24. Be honest; have you ever read verse 24 before?

I ask that because Romans 3:23 is a key verse in the Christian faith. I could have probably told you "all have sinned and fall short of the glory of God" before I understood what any of those eleven words mean. As is so often the case in Christianity, if you don't study the Scriptures, you may find yourself memorizing halves of sentences and leaving off the most important and life-changing parts.

REREAD ROMANS 3:23-24. What good news do we find in verse 24?

We are justified! We are made absolutely sinless before God. Not by following the law. Not by being super pretty or super smart or super nice or having a super empty shame reel. We are justified by the grace of God through the redemption that is in Christ Jesus.

Look back at the shame messages you wrote out on page 109. How can you rewrite those messages because of Jesus? Use these verses to help you if you get stuck: John 15:15; Romans 8:17; 2 Corinthians 5:17; Colossians 3:12; 1 Peter 2:9.

Today, pray that the Lord will keep you from living for the law, from worshiping your self and your will. Ask Him to flood you with the knowledge and joy that you are justified. You do not have to live ashamed of your past sins or ashamed of the gospel.

SPECIAL GUESTS

ROMANS 5:1-11; 6:1-2

Imagine this: Your favorite singer or band is putting on a surprise concert in your city. Your best friend just called into a radio show that she listens to every morning, trying to be the eleventh caller so she could win VIP tickets. And somehow, she wins!

Though you're listening to the show and hear her on air, you can't help but squeal when she calls to tell you the good news. But then she asks you a question you've been dying to hear: Would you like go with me?

Of course, you say yes.

You have special access to the sound check, a spectacular view of the show, and even get a private meet-and-greet after—plus your favorite item from the merch table. Although your friend was the one to win the tickets, you experience the same benefits as if you'd won because you're her friend, she chose to invite you, and you said yes.

That's what happens to us, but on the scale of infinity, when we become the children of the Creator of literally everything. We have access to the kingdom of God, not because we are incredible but because we said yes to Him. We are His.

READ ROMANS 5:1-5. Why do we have peace with God?

In verse 2, what (rather, whom) does our faith give us access to?

Being a child of God means we get access to Him, His kingdom, His friendship. It's better than winning VIP concert tickets and meeting your favorite singer backstage. Access to God means peace and hope and fulfillment. Access to God means freedom from fear and pain and sin and shame! Daughter of God, that is for you. HE is for you. Like Paul writes in verse 5, our hope will not disappoint us because God is more than just a cool thing or a cool person; He IS love, and He pours that love into our hearts through His Spirit. Wow.

CONTINUE READING VERSES 6-11. When did Christ die for the ungodly?

What does it mean for us that Christ died for us while we were still sinners?

God didn't wait until we earned our worthiness. He didn't wait until next week when we get our acts together. He didn't look around and say, "Okay, now everyone is good enough for me to send Jesus." Christ died for us while we were still sinners. While we still bore our shame and guilt and ungodliness and unworthiness.

What does verse 11 say we boast in?

Boasting in our afflictions and boasting in God may sound very different at first. How do we boast in both?

When we boast in our afflictions, we do so because we know God uses them to refine us. And, like we learned last week, we know that because of Jesus, we will not be crushed by them. Instead, they will produce hope in us. Boasting in that hope is boasting in God—the One who makes all things new, who is our hope.

READ ROMANS 6:1-2. What question did Paul ask and answer in these verses?

What a gift that our sin is forgiven and our shame is conquered. But Paul reminds us here not to live like it doesn't matter what we do once we're in Christ. We are set free from shame, and so we can live for God's glory—not in an effort to earn anything but because we love Him and our obedience and desire for righteousness reflects that.

So, are you starting to see it? Are you starting to see whatever it is that brings you shame shrink down in light of this gift? Whatever it is, it can't compare to the authority of God. And God says it is gone. So we don't brag about our ability to avoid the bad stuff that makes us feel ashamed—we brag about the God who has made us no longer shameful. Instead, He's made us His.

> *Today, pray to God like you're talking to a friend.*
> *If you've made the decision to follow Jesus, God is your friend!*
> *You don't have to avoid Him when you fail. You can*
> *bring whatever you are and whatever you've done to Him,*
> *knowing with confidence that He can handle it; He has*
> *handled it. Talk to Him, trusting that He will not shut you*
> *out or turn you away or humiliate you.*

THE SOLUTION

ROMANS 8:1-11

Many years ago, the Southern Baptist association of Miami, Florida, gave land to start a hospital called Baptist Hospital. Apparently, that donation included the agreement that Southern Baptist pastors would not have to pay for medical services in that hospital.

Decades after that transaction, I had a baby in that hospital—and the bill was something like fifteen thousand dollars. At that time, it might as well have been fifteen million dollars. We couldn't pay it. But one of the pastors my husband worked with told us, "Call the Baptist hospital, ask for the billing office, tell them that you're a Southern Baptist pastor, and they will wipe away your debt."

We couldn't believe it, but we called them and told them our situation. About thirty seconds later, they said, "Okay, your account is at zero."

If we have accepted the work of Jesus in our place, that is what happens with the debt of our sin and shame. We just ask for our account to be cleared. "God, I heard that Jesus already took the punishment for my sin, and He's already canceled my shame; will You forgive it?" And the answer is always yes because the work is already done.

We can't understand all the benefits we have from God if we don't understand our guilt and if we don't know how to release it in Him.

READ ROMANS 8:1- 4. If you're new to Christianity, it's a lot of big words and potentially confusing language, I know. I don't want that to trip you up.

> Read the first four verses slowly in whatever Bible you're using, and then write down anything that stands out to you below.

Here is that same passage in a translation that might be easier to understand.

The Solution Is Life on God's Terms

With the arrival of Jesus, the Messiah, that fateful dilemma is resolved. Those who enter into Christ's being-here-for-us no longer have to live under a continuous, low-lying black cloud. A new power is in operation. The Spirit of life in Christ, like a strong wind, has magnificently cleared the air, freeing you from a fated lifetime of brutal tyranny at the hands of sin and death.

God went for the jugular when he sent his own Son. He didn't deal with the problem as something remote and unimportant. In his Son, Jesus, he personally took on the human condition, entered the disordered mess of struggling humanity in order to set it right once and for all. The law code, weakened as it always was by fractured human nature, could never have done that.

The law always ended up being used as a Band-Aid on sin instead of a deep healing of it. And now what the law code asked for but we couldn't deliver is accomplished as we, instead of redoubling our own efforts, simply embrace what the Spirit is doing in us.

ROMANS 8:1-4, THE MESSAGE

I don't know Greek or Hebrew (don't worry, the editors of this study do), so I love looking at the same passage in multiple translations. (You can do this free online at biblegateway.com, blueletterbible.org, and biblehub.com.)

Seeing the same thing said in a new way often helps it click for me. The law was a Band-Aid®, but Jesus Christ heals us deeply. "Redoubling our efforts" is not going to take away from how badly we've messed everything up. Embracing the Spirit is what will make us new. How beautiful.

When have you tried to "redouble your efforts" instead of giving something over to God?

The law in this case was referring to the law God gave Moses in the Old Testament. The Jewish people were still looking to the law for salvation and instructions for right living. Jesus came to fulfill the law for us (Matt. 5:17).

What has it looked like in your own life when you tried to live by the law?

When did you realize you couldn't do it?

Today we don't often think of the law of Moses, but we do often try to live by our own set of rules, whether that means the law of the government, what we consider to be the rules of being a good Christian, or a set of demands we've created in our own minds to live right.

If you had to write out ten "rules" that describe the way you live your life, what would they be?

What would you say rests at the heart of your rules? Why?

READ ROMANS 8:5-11. What is the mindset of the Spirit?

What hope! We are no longer in the flesh if we have made the decision to follow Christ. We have life and peace. While our bodies will still experience death here on earth, we have a future resurrection to look forward to and a present life of abundance to live in now (John 10:10).

What are the most meaningful ways you have embraced the Spirit who makes you new?

Today, pray that God will help you embrace and enjoy life in His Spirit. Ask Him to help you turn from striving and trying to be good on your own. Ask Him to forgive your mistakes and make you into a more joyful, more peaceful worshiper of Him.

REASSURANCE FOR US LITTLE CHILDREN

1 JOHN 2:28-29; 3:1-24

Becoming a mom has changed how I think about the second coming. Here's what I mean. Today, as I'm finishing up the draft of this study, my youngest daughter has been learning to knit a scarf. It's not a perfect scarf, but she did improbably great on her first try. Seeing her wear it is too adorable. And this afternoon, all I wanted in the world was for her to succeed at her first attempt at knitting. Because her sadness is my sadness. Her frustrations are mine. Her pain gives me pain. I would never watch my baby knit and hope for the worst. I only hope for the best. I want to see her thrive. I want to see her joyful. I want to see her knit with the power of a thousand grannies. So, I would never, ever wish for her to fail. I don't watch her try things hoping for a chance to call her out. I love her. She's mine. And I'm an imperfect mom. I'm a flawed knitter nurturer.

But our God is a perfect Father. So, please let this into your heart: God is not waiting for you to mess up. He's not hoping to see you sin right before He comes again. When He comes in the clouds, it won't be a cosmic-level "gotcha" for all His followers who failed most recently. He's not hanging out in heaven waiting for you to botch your scarf before He blows the trumpet and returns to shame you. Your sadness is His sadness. Your pain does not go unnoticed. God cares for the brokenhearted (Ps. 34:18).

He loves us. We're His. So I love how John addresses his readers as "little children" in his letter. Yes, God has the right to judge all the evil and all the failure in the world, and He will. But the judge is our Dad. We are His little daughters. He wants to see us thrive forever. Amazing.

READ 1 JOHN 2:28-29. According to these verses, what are we supposed to do so that we are not "ashamed" when Christ returns?

READ 1 JOHN 3:1-3. What does verse 1 show us is the great love of God?

What do we know about everyone who has this hope in God based on verse 3?

We who are children of God are pure. We're pure! No matter how dirty your life has been, no matter how dark, no matter how far you've walked from God. No matter what you can remember from your past. If you are His child, He purifies you like He is pure.

READ I JOHN 3:4-10. Do these verses feel confusing or contradictory in light of what you just read in verses 1-3? Explain.

These verses can be confusing if you're a former or current striver, like me. I remember being baffled and anxious when Jesus or His disciples wrote about how we are to live as children of God. I'm going to mess that up! I've already messed that up!

In what areas of your life have you felt like you've messed up recently?

But you have to remember the overarching message of the gospel, which is that we cannot and did not earn our purity. It was a free gift, and because we have been so loved, so forgiven, and so blessed, the Spirit of God changes us and makes us holier.

How does it comfort you to know that no amount or level of mess-ups can remove God's children from His capable hands?

My husband has often preached, "If you read God's Word and don't feel hopeful, keep reading."

So, let's keep reading. **READ I JOHN 3:11-24.** What does John urge us "little children" to do in verse 18?

Our good works are a sign of our salvation, not a means to it. John is urging believers to live out our position in Jesus, not like the Jewish religious leaders of the day who knew the law and could speak the law but didn't live the law. No. Real believers will love "in action and in truth." It is a result of our conversion. It's a result of God's love for us. Let's keep reading.

REWRITE I JOHN 3:19-20 in big bold letters in the space below. Underline what will happen to our hearts.

I'm going to type it out and underline it here, too.

> _This is how we will know that we belong to the truth and will_
> _reassure our hearts before him whenever our hearts condemn_
> _us; for God is greater than our hearts, and he knows all things._

I don't know about you, but when I battle shame, what I long for most is reassurance. I want to know that I'm okay. I want to know that the shame I'm wrestling with today doesn't condemn me.

So, how can we be reassured? It's right there in your handwriting: GOD IS GREATER THAN OUR HEARTS. When your heart condemns you, God says, "There is now no condemnation for those in Christ Jesus" (Rom. 8:1).

Who is greater? No-brainer. God is greater than your heart. He's greater than your memories, your shame, your internal condemnation. He wants to interrupt your shame reel with a commercial of Jesus saying, "It is finished" (John 19:30). God is always greater than your heart. And the more you reflect on that, the more your life will reflect Jesus's life, and as it does, you will see and know and be reassured that you are a child of God.

Consider writing out those verses on an index card or sticky note and placing it wherever your shame reel starts playing in your head—your mirror, your car dashboard, your bedroom door—as a reminder that God is greater.

READ I JOHN 3:21-24. What are we commanded to do?

> _Close out this day reflecting on what it might_
> _look like for you to obey God today. Walking in a_
> _relationship with Jesus leads to obedience._
> _Obedience leads to joy and reassurance. There's no_
> _more room for shame when you're full of joy._

IN A CLOUD OF RIGHTEOUS COMPANY

HEBREWS 11:32–12:3

READ HEBREWS 11:32-40. Do you recognize any of those Bible names from the Old Testament? What do you remember about them besides what was listed in these verses?

What does verse 39 say they were approved "through"?

Like me, you might have heard Bible stories growing up and viewed all the people as heroes. But if you actually read their stories, they had big-time failures too. Tons to be ashamed of. First on that list is Gideon. We usually stop talking about him after God used him to defeat the Midianites. But do you know how his story ended? Check out Judges 8:27:

> Gideon made an ephod from all this and put it in Ophrah, his hometown. Then all Israel prostituted themselves by worshiping it there, and it became a snare to Gideon and his household.

Gideon got to rescue God's people, then his life ended shamefully and "the Israelites did not remember the LORD their God who had rescued them from the hand of the enemies around them" (v. 34). That's not just the end of Gideon's shame reel, that's the end of his life reel.

David, number five on the list, was an adulterer who had someone murdered. But, of course, he also defeated a giant through God's power and won victories for God's people.

The "Hall of Faith" is filled with failure-heroes. This is such a relief, isn't it? We can be used big time for God even though we fail. Shameful moments don't disqualify us. Jesus's perfection qualifies us.

> When have you been tempted to think your shameful moments disqualify you from being used by God? How does this passage show you a different picture?

And that is the incredible reality we have in Jesus. Because of Jesus, we can have a powerful impact in this world. But because of Jesus, we don't actually have to save the day. Jesus has already saved the day. Jesus is mighty enough to lead us to incredible impact, and Jesus is mighty enough to cover incredible failures. Our approval then is based on the Object of our faith, not our perfect track record.

> **LOOK AT HEBREWS 12:1-3.** The writer of Hebrews urges us to do a few things in light of this great "cloud of witnesses" he just wrote about in chapter 11. What does he say to do? Finish these sentences.
>
> We are to lay aside _____.
>
>
>
> We are to run with _____.
>
>
>
> We are to keep our eyes on _____.

Now, personalize it. What could it practically look like to do those three things in your life?

How does it encourage you to have this cloud of witnesses—these failure-heroes—surrounding you?

Do you have a modern-day cloud of witnesses? Do you have friends who are walking alongside you, cheering you on, and pointing you to Jesus? If so, who are they and how have they encourage you? If not, what are steps you can take this week to work toward building one?

How can you be the one who points others to Jesus as you run alongside them?

Jesus is the pioneer and perfecter of our faith. He wore your shame and suffered your punishment and conquered it. He is at God's right hand right now (Rom. 8:34), preparing a place for you (John 14:2).

> *Your shame was crucified when Jesus was. It's finished.*
> *Our hope was established when He rose from the dead. Hallelujah!*
> *We don't have to live with shame. We are forgiven.*

SESSION 6 / GROUP TIME

WATCH

Write down any thoughts, verses, or things you want to remember as you watch the video for Session Six.

To access the video teaching sessions, use the instructions in the back of your Bible study book.

DISCUSS

This week, we looked at shame and why we don't have to live enslaved to it. New Testament writers, inspired by the Holy Spirit, reminded us that we are justified and pure and righteous because of our faith in Jesus. Is this concept difficult for you to grasp or remember? Why or why not?

This session's main idea is "Jesus experienced our shame so we don't have to." Take a few minutes to talk about what that means and why it matters for us today.

On Day Five, you personalized Hebrews 12:1-3. What can living out those verses look like for you, and what might it look like for our group?

What is the number one thing you have taken away from this study over the past six weeks?

> THEREFORE, SINCE WE ALSO HAVE SUCH A LARGE CLOUD OF WITNESSES SURROUNDING US, LET US LAY ASIDE EVERY HINDRANCE AND THE SIN THAT SO EASILY ENSNARES US. LET US RUN WITH ENDURANCE THE RACE THAT LIES BEFORE US, KEEPING OUR EYES ON JESUS, THE PIONEER AND PERFECTER OF OUR FAITH. FOR THE JOY THAT LAY BEFORE HIM, HE ENDURED THE CROSS, DESPISING THE SHAME, AND SAT DOWN AT THE RIGHT HAND OF THE THRONE OF GOD.
>
> **HEBREWS 12:1-2**

PRAY

Thank God for His Word and its shame-fighting power. Ask that He'd continue the good work He's done in you and your group as you continue to walk with Him.

APPENDIX

BECOMING A CHRISTIAN

Romans 10:17 says, "So faith comes from what is heard, and what is heard comes through the message about Christ."

Maybe you've stumbled across new information in this study. Maybe you've attended church all your life, but something you read here struck you differently than it has before. Or maybe you are exhausted from wrestling with shame, and you are looking for the rest and peace that can only come from casting your cares on Jesus, who cares for you. If you have never accepted Christ but would like to, read on to discover how you can become a Christian.

Your heart tends to run from God and rebel against Him. The Bible calls this sin. Romans 3:23 says, "For all have sinned and fall short of the glory of God."

Yet God loves you and wants to save you from sin, to offer you a new life of hope. John 10:10b says, "I have come so that they may have life and have it in abundance."

To give you this gift of salvation, God made a way through His Son, Jesus Christ. Romans 5:8 says, "But God proves his own love for us in that while we were still sinners, Christ died for us."

You receive this gift by faith alone. Ephesians 2:8-9 says, "For you are saved by grace through faith, and this is not from yourselves; it is God's gift—not from works, so that no one can boast."

Faith is a decision of your heart demonstrated by the actions of your life. Romans 10:9 says, "If you confess with your mouth, 'Jesus is Lord,' and believe in your heart that God raised him from the dead, you will be saved."

If you trust that Jesus died for your sins and want to receive new life through Him, pray a prayer similar to the following one to express your repentance and faith in Him.

> Dear God, I know I am a sinner. I believe Jesus died to forgive me of my sins. I accept Your offer of eternal life. Thank You for forgiving me of all my sins. Thank You for my new life. From this day forward, I will choose to follow You.

If you have trusted Jesus for salvation, please share your decision with your group leader or another Christian friend. If you are not already attending church, find one where you can worship and grow in your faith. Following Christ's example, ask to be baptized as a public expression of your faith.

SCARLET'S
FAVORITE
SHAME FIGHTING
VERSES

A lot of these verses have been pulled from what we've studied the last few weeks, so you know some of the context. If a verse is new to you (or even if you have heard it before), I encourage you to read the context around the verse. That way, you can more fully understand what it is about. This is the Word of God! Put these in your pocket. Tape them to your mirrors. Set them as the lock-screen on your phone. This is truth. These words have power. This is how we fight.

. . . .

But you, LORD, are a shield around me,
my glory, and the one who lifts up my head.

PSALM 3:3

. . . .

4 I sought the LORD, and he answered me
and rescued me from all my fears.
5 Those who look to him are radiant with joy;
their faces will never be ashamed.

PSALM 34:4-5

. . . .

As far as the east is from the west,
so far has he removed
our transgressions from us.

PSALM 103:12

. . . .

*The Lord G*OD *will help me;*
therefore I have not been humiliated;
therefore I have set my face like flint,
and I know I will not be put to shame.

ISAIAH 50:7

⁴ *"Do not be afraid, for you will not be put to shame;*
don't be humiliated, for you will not be disgraced.
For you will forget the shame of your youth,
and you will no longer remember
the disgrace of your widowhood.
⁵ *Indeed, your husband is your Maker—*
*his name is the L*ORD *of Armies—*
and the Holy One of Israel is your Redeemer;
he is called the God of the whole earth.
⁶ *For the L*ORD *has called you,*
like a wife deserted and wounded in spirit,
a wife of one's youth when she is rejected,"
says your God.
⁷ *"I deserted you for a brief moment,*
but I will take you back with abundant compassion.
⁸ *In a surge of anger*
I hid my face from you for a moment,
but I will have compassion on you
with everlasting love,"
*says the L*ORD *your Redeemer.*

ISAIAH 54:4-8

In place of your shame, you will have a double portion;

in place of disgrace, they will rejoice over their share.

So they will possess double in their land,

and eternal joy will be theirs.

ISAIAH 61:7

He will again have compassion on us;

he will vanquish our iniquities.

You will cast all our sins into the depths of the sea.

MICAH 7:19

Therefore, there is now no condemnation

for those in Christ Jesus.

ROMANS 8:1

For the Scripture says, Everyone who believes

on him will not be put to shame.

ROMANS 10:11

For godly grief produces a repentance that leads to salvation without regret, but worldly grief produces death.

2 CORINTHIANS 7:10

How much more will the blood of Christ, who through the eternal Spirit offered himself without blemish to God, cleanse our consciences from dead works so that we can serve the living God?

HEBREWS 9:14

Let us draw near with a true heart in full assurance of faith, with our hearts sprinkled clean from an evil conscience and our bodies washed in pure water.

HEBREWS 10:22

. . . keeping our eyes on Jesus, the pioneer and perfecter of our faith. For the joy that lay before him, he endured the cross, despising the shame, and sat down at the right hand of the throne of God.

HEBREWS 12:2

But if anyone suffers as a Christian, let him not be ashamed but let him glorify God in having that name.

1 PETER 4:16

ENDNOTES

SESSION TWO

1. Strong's H5771: aôn, Blue Letter Bible, accessed May 22, 2023, https://www.blueletterbible.org/lexicon/h5771/csb/wlc/0-1/.
2. Andrew M. Davis, *Exalting Jesus in Isaiah* (Nashville, TN: Holman Reference, 2017), 41.
3. J. R. R. Tolkien, *The Return of the King* (New York: Harper Collins, 1967), 283.
4. A. W. Tozer, *The Knowledge of the Holy* (New York: HarperOne, 1961), 70.

SESSION THREE

1. D. A. Carson, *The Gospel According to John, The Pillar New Testament Commentary* (Leicester, England; Grand Rapids, MI: Inter-Varsity Press; W.B. Eerdmans, 1991), 216.

SESSION FOUR

1. Thabiti Anyabwile, *Christ-Centered Exposition Commentary: Exalting Jesus in Luke* (Nashville: B&H Publishing Group, 2018).
2. A. Boyd Luter, "Galatians," in *CSB Study Bible: Notes*, ed. Edwin A. Blum and Trevin Wax (Nashville, TN: Holman Bible Publishers, 2017), 1860.
3. Edward T. Welch, *When People are Big and God is Small* (Phillipsburg, New Jersey: P & R Publishing, 2023), ch. 1.
4. Ashley Hamer, "Here's Why Smells Trigger Such Vivid Memories," *Discovery*, August 1, 2019, https://www.discovery.com/science/Why-Smells-Trigger-Such-Vivid-Memories.
5. Timothy Keller, *The Reason for God* (New York: Penguin Books, 2008), ch. 11.

LEADER GUIDE

TIPS FOR LEADING A GROUP

PRAY DILIGENTLY. Ask God to prepare you to lead this study. Pray individually and specifically for the girls in your group. Make this a priority in your personal walk and preparation.

PREPARE ADEQUATELY. Don't just wing this. Take time to preview each week so you have a good grasp of the content. Look over the group session and consider those in your group. Feel free to delete or reword the questions provided, and add questions that better fit your group.

LEAD BY EXAMPLE. Make sure you complete all of the personal study. Be willing to share your story, what you're learning, and your questions as you discuss together.

BE AWARE. If girls are hesitant to discuss their thoughts and questions in a larger group, consider dividing into smaller groups to provide a setting more conducive to conversation.

FOLLOW UP. If someone mentions a prayer request or need, make sure to follow up. It may be a situation where you can get others in the group involved in helping out.

EVALUATE OFTEN. After each week and throughout the study, assess what needs to be changed to more effectively lead the study.

MAKE THE MOST OF YOUR GROUP TIME

WELCOME

Help ease into each session by starting off with some questions to get girls comfortable with one another. After Session One, this will be a great time to review the previous week's main theme, memory verse, and personal study. Pray together before you watch the video.

WATCH

You'll find detailed information on how to access the teaching videos in the back of your Bible study book. You may choose to watch them individually or as a group before you begin discussion. Encourage your girls to use the space in their books to take notes. It will be extremely helpful for you, as the leader, to watch the videos ahead of Group Time to best be prepared for discussion.

In the Session 5 video, the author covers topics that could be difficult for some teen girls. These topics include grief (throughout the video), suicide (4:00–4:07), and eating disorders (5:40–5:45). As you work through the video for this week, please preview the content beforehand and take into consideration the needs of each of the girls in your group before showing the video in its entirety.

DISCUSS

The last page of each session includes key ideas and questions to help you lead meaningful discussions with your girls. But don't stress if you don't cover all the info or answer all the questions. Your goal is to help your girls move beyond surface-level answers to see what God's Word teaches them about shame, understand themselves better in light of what His Word says about them, and connect with other girls who can encourage them in their faith and their fight against shame.

RELEASE

- Challenge girls to memorize next week's theme and memory verse as they study.
- Encourage girls to complete as much of the five personal days as they can on their own before each session. Between your group times, check in with girls on how they are doing and ask if they have questions about what they are studying.
- Close with prayer, using the prompt on the discuss page.

BE PRESENT

Shame can be a really difficult topic, especially for teen girls, who may feel shame for all sorts of reasons—even reasons they don't understand. Make yourself available to listen, ask how they're feeling throughout the week, and point them to God-honoring resources and counselors as needed.

MOM & DAUGHTER GUIDE

Mom, we are so excited that you have decided to complete this study with your daughter. As Scarlet Hiltibidal walks you through what God's Word says about shame, you will find an invitation for both you and your daughter to see where shame comes from, to understand how Jesus frees us from our shame, and to see how to erase your shame reel and live in that freedom.

YOU WILL NEED

- *Ashamed: Women's Bible Study Book* for yourself (with video access code)
- *Ashamed: Teen Girls' Bible Study Book* for your daughter(s)

VIDEO CONTENT

The weekly videos that are included in the Bible study book can be watched with your daughter during the Group Time sessions. Follow the instructions in the back of your Bible study book to access the teaching videos.

STUDY

As you begin each session, you will spend time working through the Group Time found in the *Ashamed: Teen Girls' Bible Study Book*. The discussion questions will help you go deeper as you review your personal study.

As you both work through your individual Bible study books, you will discover that the teen girls' version might be slightly different as we altered some language and content to be more applicable for teen girls.

However, there are very few differences in the studies, and we encourage you to discuss what the Lord is teaching you individually.

CONNECT WITH HER

Plan days to work on personal study together to keep each other accountable. Be open with your daughter throughout the week about things you learn or have questions about. Provide a safe place for her to do the same. Don't stress! Some weeks will be easier than others to accomplish the personal study days. Just keep pressing forward and making it a priority to meet together each week regardless of how much personal study work was actually done.

FAQ

Q: How old does my teen need to be for this study?

A: This study is recommended for girls ages 11 and up.

Q: Are there other studies I can do with my daughter after this study is over?

A: Yes! Many of our studies have both women's and teen girls' materials available.

CHECK IT OUT AT
LIFEWAY.COM/GIRLS

IF YOU'RE STUCK IN SHAME . . .

There's no shame in that. But really—learning to lean into God and fight shame like a pro takes time. Here are some good resources to help you keep fighting and overcome shame.

USE SCARLET'S FAVORITE SHAME FIGHTING VERSES ON PAGES 130-134. Shame comes from sin and our experiences living in a fallen world, but shame also comes from the lies we tell ourselves about ourselves and the world around us. We feel what we feel—that's valid. But sometimes our feelings lie to us about what's really happening. Knowing God's Word, knowing the ultimate truth, helps us beat back the lies. We can "take every thought captive" in Christ, holding it up against the truth of God's Word to see if what we're thinking or feeling is what's actually happening (2 Cor. 10:5).

TRY WRITING IT OUT. Sometimes seeing something written out in our own handwriting helps us see it in a new light. Grab a journal and get curious. Use these questions to guide your journaling:
- What do I believe that is leading me to feel shame?
- What's keeping me stuck here?
- Does what I believe about this situation seem fact-based or is it feelings-based? Is it well-balanced or extreme?
- How does what I believe/think/feel line up with God's Word? What are some specific verses that can help me in this situation?
- Now that I've examined what I believe about the situation as well as what God's Word says, how can I rewrite my initial idea about the situation?

REACH OUT. It takes courage to speak up when you're struggling, but it's so important. Shame grows in silence. If you're struggling with shame and don't know where to turn or need help navigating the process of finding a counselor, reach out to someone you trust to talk about what's going on in your life—a parent, a small group leader or mentor, a friend. God didn't design us to walk through life on earth alone—we were made to stand together and encourage each other as we fulfill God's plan for us.

FIND A GODLY COUNSELOR. Use resources like aacc.net, focusonthefamily.com/counseling, and biblicalcounseling.com. These websites will provide names of Christian counselors in your area. If you need or want to find a counselor through telehealth options, you can also use a resource like betterhelp.com and specify that you want to work with a Christian counselor. You can also ask your youth pastor or other church leaders for their recommendations. If you need help walking through this process, ask a parent or other trusted adult.

MOST OF ALL, REMEMBER THAT JESUS DEFEATED SIN AND SHAME ON THE CROSS, AND SHAME HAS NO POWER OVER YOU, DAUGHTER OF GOD.

THERE ARE MANY REASONS TO WORRY. AND ONE REASON NOT TO.

The world we live in can be overwhelming—full of brokenness and uncertainty. Yet the Bible assures us that Jesus entered the broken, sad, and scary places to rescue and love us, offering the only true solution and protection. Join Scarlet Hiltibidal in this 8-session study to learn how we can practically take hold of the perfect peace that is only available through God as we dive deeply into His Word, embrace the practice of prayer, and live authentically in the support of our communities of faith.

Bible Study Book with Video Access   005829921 $19.99

LIFEWAY.COM/ANXIOUS

ALSO AVAILABLE FROM
SCARLET HILTIBIDAL

FOR TEENS

Available wherever books are sold

B&H PUBLISHING

Get the most from your study.

eBook with video access, includes 6 video teaching sessions from Scarlet Hiltibidal, each approximately 7 minutes

IN THIS STUDY, YOU'LL:

- Gain perspective on sources of shame and grasp a vision for how to find freedom through God's Word.
- Experience the miraculous shift of living in light of the gospel today rather than hoping for a happy someday.
- Learn from the stories of women and men in the Bible who overcame their shame to walk in the freedom of God.

To enrich your study experience, consider the accompanying video teaching sessions from Scarlet Hiltibidal, approximately 7 minutes each.

STUDYING ON YOUR OWN?

Watch Scarlet Hiltibidal's teaching sessions, available via redemption code for individual video-streaming access, printed in this Bible study book.

LEADING A GROUP?

Each group member will need an *Ashamed* study book, which includes video access. Because all participants will have access to the video content, you can choose to watch the videos outside of your group meeting if desired. Or, if you're watching together and someone misses a group meeting, they'll have the flexibility to catch up!

Browse a free session sample, social media assets, video clips, church promotional materials, and more at

lifeway.com/ashamed